REGENER8

8 weeks
8 lessons
8 truths

Straight Talk for
Street Smart Teens

ROBERT COOK

REGENER8: STRAIGHT TALK FOR
STREET SMART TEENS BY ROBERT COOK
Published by Lighthouse Publishing of the Carolinas
2333 Barton Oaks Dr., Raleigh, NC, 27614

ISBN 978-1-938499-08-1

Available in print from your local bookstore, online, or from the publisher at:
www.lighthousepublishingofthecarolinas.com

For more information on this book and the author visit:
www.facebook.com/Regener8

Library of Congress Cataloging-in-Publication Data
Cook, Robert.
Regener8: Straight Talk for Street Smart Teens / Robert Cook 1st ed.

Printed in the United States of America

**Lighthouse Publishing
of the Carolinas**

Contents

Robt Cook

Mark 2:17

REGENER8

8 weeks   8 lessons   8 truths

Robt Cook

Mark 2:17

Foreword

There is a very familiar story in the Gospels where Jesus showed up at a pool surrounded by people with physical maladies. Every so often the angel would stir the waters and whoever got to the water first was healed. As Jesus gazed across the multitude of people in various stages of suffering and death, He stooped to talk to one man who had been paralyzed for 38 years. "Would you like to walk?" Christ asked the man. "How can I? When the water stirs, someone always beats me to the pool." Jesus reaches down and heals the man. This story has always bothered me. In thirty-eight years of healings in the water, why didn't anyone go back to help others into the pool?

That is exactly what Rob Cook is doing. He, much like myself, languished in sin and strongholds. Jesus healed Rob and daily Rob goes back to the pool to help others receive the healing waters of salvation. This book is a great tool for anyone, especially students and young adults who have been by the pool of sin and stronghold, who have been wrecked by the world. In the pages of this little book you will learn to walk and think as Jesus did. I am grateful to God for how He is using Rob to reach many of those our society has forgotten. May God shine mercy and favor on Regener8 and Rob's ministry to students and young adults.

~ Dr. Chris Stephens,
Senior Pastor, Faith Promise Church,
Knoxville, TN

Introduction

All I can say is, no way. I can't believe you're reading this book. Not that I am surprised that you can actually read; I'm just surprised I actually finished it. I'm not the only one shocked, either. Pretty much everyone who knows me is blown away.

Let's just say that I'm not famous for following through. In fact, if a writing career doesn't pan out, I'm seriously considering being the poster child for ADD. I wonder if that pays well.

Don't get me wrong; I always have good intentions. That's not the issue. The real problem is that I soon grow bored with whatever project I'm doing, and I move on. My office is filled with perfectly good story ideas that have fizzled out around page 100 for no other reason than that my mind has 1,000 ideas at once, and I jump around a lot.

With REGENER8, however, it was different. It was important. I needed to finish it for you.

Although this book is for young people from all walks of life, my heart resonates with young people from broken homes and dysfunctional families.

If you live in either group, or both of them, my heart goes out to you. I came from a broken home and lived with a physically abusive, alcoholic father.

I didn't fit in with the "in" crowd. My friends and I hid on the fringes of society. We were labeled outcasts, troubled kids, and my personal favorite, juvenile delinquents.

We were not jocks. We were not popular. The streets felt like home.

Adults disapproved of everything we loved: the way we dressed, the way we talked, the music we listened to. The list was endless. They wrote us off, and we didn't care. Or at least we acted like we didn't care. We felt unloved and unwanted.

We did what we wanted, when we wanted. Unfortunately, when you live life by your own rules, you tend to break others.

This led to multiple run-ins with authoritative types who usually wore blue uniforms and had pretty shiny matching bracelets that they were all too happy to let us wear.

Some of my friends were not as lucky as I was. Their stories ended in long prison sentences, death from drug or alcohol over-doses, shootings, or suicide.

It's only by the grace of God I sit here and write to you. God had a purpose for me, although I didn't know it or care about it back then. I had my reasons.

My mom forced me to go to church, and I heard all about how God loved me and how we need to love each other and not judge people. But those same people at that church did not seem to love me. And they judged me. I didn't fit into the mold of what they thought a "Christian" should look like.

I figured if that was the God they served, they could keep Him to themselves.

They had too many rules anyway. And their rules and my rules did not get along.

I was shocked when, years later, I found out that God was

nothing like they made Him out to be. God called people like them *hypocrites*. He wasn't pleased with them or their self-righteous attitudes.

What I learned about the real God of the Bible radically changed my life.

That life-changing discovery is the foundation of this book.

I feel compelled to set the record straight. I want you to have the facts, not hypocritical opinions. I wanted you to have the knowledge of Jesus without man's imposed restrictions.

I want you to meet the real God. I want you to make an informed decision for yourself.

God does not care what you look like. He does not care what you've done, where you've been, what you've said, or what music you listen to.

He loves you and wants to have a relationship with you, and He gave His life to prove it.

For the next eight weeks, let's journey together through the Gospel, and see the unconditional love God has for each of us, and what He really wants from you.

I am going to team up with you. If you have any questions while you're reading this book, you can contact me personally at *rcook252underground@gmail.com*.

On the seventh day of each week, you will find Teen Take. Real, unedited, in their own words, teen stories, describing how they overcame their challenges.

I pray that, like them, you will overcome yours.

REGENER8

Truth about Porn

Week 1 Day 1

Sexedemic: I coined this term to describe the sex epidemic facing our nation.

Sex is "in your face" everywhere, trying to convince you it's the acceptable way of doing business.

Don't believe it? They've got a hot babe in a barely-there bikini hawking the latest skateboard gear. What about the girl in the thong with the strategically-placed guitar to hide her silicone implants? What does that have to do with guitar strings?

You've seen the ads but probably never gave them a second thought.

HERE'S WHY

This is nothing new. They didn't just drop this on you. It's a well-calculated strategy to desensitize your mind and influence your thoughts.

By the time you're a teenager, you've been subjected to thousands of sexual images. Your mind is numb, so you embrace it as normal. Mission accomplished.

RIGHT WHERE THEY WANT YOU

So now you've bought into their twisted logic. You get a smart phone and you can view porn 24/7 in HD color and sound. Anywhere, anytime you want, but you wait until you're alone and do it in secret.

WHY?

Because a part of you screams it's wrong. You're ashamed, so you hide it. You look good as long as no one knows.

HERE'S THE BAD NEWS

God knows. Don't believe in God? He still knows.

You think Criss Angel is a mind freak? Check this: God knows your every thought.

Here's what Jesus says about your little "secret":

> "You have heard that it was said, 'Do not commit adultery.' But I tell you that anyone who looks at a woman lustfully has already committed adultery with her in his heart."
>
> (Matthew 5:27 NIV)

Get your mind out of the gutter.
Your heart will follow.

Week 1 Day 2

YUCK!

So picture this.

You're chillin' with your posse and you see your bud chompin' some gum. You ask for a piece. He says sure and takes the piece he's chewing out of his mouth.

NOT WHAT YOU HAD IN MIND

Is he trippin'? You want a fresh piece, not some slobbered on, no flavor left, ABC (already been chewed) piece.

Think about your future wife, the mother of your children. What do you think she'd want? Stop playin'. You know the answer.

It might not mean that much now but think about it: On your honeymoon, do you wanna be with someone who's slept with 30 guys?

I know. Stupid question, right?

Turn the tables. Would that beautiful woman next to you be happy with the knowledge that you slept with half your high school? Another stupid question, right?

KEEP YOUR PANTS ON

It's about respect. Don't put yourself in a position where things get hot and heavy and you're not thinking straight because, trust me, by then it's too late. It's like closing the gate after your dog runs away.

Be proactive. Set boundaries. Being a teenager with raging hormones is hard enough. Don't make it worse.

BETTER ADVICE

Here's the Bible's take:

> "But since sexual immorality is occurring, each man should have sexual relations with his own wife, and each woman with her own husband."
>
> (1 Corinthians 7:2)

STILL NOT CONVINCED?

This might help:

> "It is God's will that you should be sanctified: that you should avoid sexual immorality; that each of you should learn to control your own body in a way that is holy and honorable, not in passionate lust like the pagans, who do not know God; and that in this matter no one should wrong or take advantage of a brother or sister. The Lord will punish all those who commit such sins, as we told you and warned you before. God did not call us to be impure, but to live a holy life. Therefore, anyone who rejects this instruction does not reject a human being but God, the very God who gives you his Holy Spirit."
>
> (1 Thessalonians 4:3-8)

Be a fresh pack of gum on your wedding night!

Week 1 Day 3

"IT'S MY BODY"

Actually, it's not. Technically, Jesus bought you when He bought it, as in took the nails for you and me. You've heard the story, I'm sure. The one where Jesus was beaten for no reason. They spit on Him and gave Him that crown of thorns you see in all the pics. Yeah, that story. The one where they hammered nails into His hands and feet and hung Him on a cross—for our sins. Guess that makes Him the first and only true BFF, 'cause, trust me, I don't care how many friends you got on Facebook®, not one of them would lay down his life for you like that.

If Jesus had a Twitter® account, this would be His tweet on the subject:

> "Do you not know that your body is a temple of the Holy Spirit," (That's God, by the way), "who is in you, whom you have received from God? You are not your own, you were bought with a price. Therefore honor God with your body."
>
> (1 Corinthians 6:19-20)

Look it up!

GOD CREATED SEX

So you're thinking, how can it be bad?

It is and it isn't.

Say what?

News flash: Sex is awesome when it's used the way God intended—between a man and his wife. That's it. Anything else is a sin. Period.

THE GOOD, THE BAD, THE UGLY

First, the good: God created man and woman to become husband and wife through the covenant of marriage. That doesn't mean living together seven years and then pulling the common law marriage card. (Nice try, though.)

The Bible says:

> "For this reason a man will leave his father and mother and be united to his wife, and they will become one flesh."
>
> (Genesis 2:24)

When you're married, sex is good in God's eyes. Yeah!

Now the bad: When we engage in sex before marriage, not only are we disobeying God, and that's bad enough, but He compares it to having sex with a prostitute.

> "The body is not meant for sexual immorality, but for the Lord, and the Lord for the body... Shall I take the members of Christ and unite them with a prostitute?"
>
> (1 Corinthians 6:13-15, author's paraphrase)

And the ugly: Flee from sexual immorality. All other sins a man commits are outside his body, but he who sins sexually sins against his own body (1 Corinthians 6:18).

BOTTOM LINE

Jesus said,

> "You have heard that it was said, 'Do not commit adultery.' But I tell you that anyone who looks at a woman lustfully has already committed adultery with her in his heart."
>
> (Matthew 5:27-28)

Let's be real. If you're viewing porn, it's lustfully, which equals adultery. And that equals sin. See how that adds up? Unfortunately, that equation does not add up to God's perfect law.

Keep your heart and mind pure.
They don't belong to you.

Week 1 Day 4

PHOTOSHOP REALITY

Talk about an oxymoron. The other negative issue with looking at porno mags or watching porn videos is that they distort your view of women. You believe all women are 36-24-36 nymphomaniacs waiting to have sex with you 24/7? Only in your dreams. They become objects to fulfill your sexual desires. These videos and magazines don't portray real women. They are just illusions created by the male ego.

HERE'S THE PROBLEM

You become delusional. You expect all women to look and act like the ones in the mags and videos. You see women as emotionless sex dolls.

You live in a fantasy. And when faced with reality, you will never be satisfied. You'll want the "perfect" woman you've been brainwashed to expect.

You've been played.

It's time to school you on the subject of airbrushed deception. The pictures you see of these "perfect" women with "perfect" bodies only exist in computer programs. Blemishes are erased, fat dissolved, and skin tanned to perfection. All of that happens with the click of a mouse. Sometimes those photos are so drastically altered that you'd hardly recognize those women face to face.

Check out the new Captain America movie. They put Chris Evans' head on some skinny guy's body. Same difference.

Unfortunately, we guys are not smart enough to realize we've been brainwashed. We expect this artificial standard of perfection.

BUBBLE-BURSTING WAKE-UP CALL

The average woman does not do the things portrayed in porn videos. They don't answer the door half-naked for the mailman. They are not interested in a threesome with your best friend or her girlfriend. And no, they don't want you to tape it and show it to your drunk friends.

These videos and images degrade women and destroy your ability to have a natural relationship with your future wife.

> Real men do not watch porn. Real men respect women.
>
> Real men do not treat women as objects. Real men honor their wives.
>
> Real men build healthy relationships.
>
> Are you a real man?

> This is how God expects you to treat your future wife:

> **"Husbands, love your wives, just as Christ loved the church and gave Himself up for her to make her holy, cleansing her by the washing with water through the word [the Bible] and to present her to Himself as a radiant church, without stain or wrinkle or any other**

blemish, but holy and blameless. In this same way, husbands ought to love their wives as their own bodies. He who loves his wife loves himself."

(Ephesians 5:25-28)

Be a real man.
There aren't enough of them.

Week 1 Day 5

OFF TO THE GYM

Every guy knows that girls dig muscles, so every guy wants muscles. The problem is you can't buy muscles. You have to work at it.

MC SQUARED

There's a whole scientific process to building muscles. If you want to know the process, Google® it.

Knowing the process is not the issue. *Sticking* to the process is where we often fall short. That's why most of your friends have 10-inch arms and can get on the elevator before the door opens.

We want to be ripped, but we don't want to put in the effort it takes.

If you had an instructor, a.k.a. a personal trainer, you would stand a much greater chance of reaching your goals.

He would tell you what foods to avoid and which ones to consume for maximum results. He would set a strict daily workout regimen for you to follow. He would push you beyond your limits. He would hold you accountable and remind you of your goals. If you followed in his footsteps, over time you would gain the physique you desired.

COMMON SENSE

When choosing a personal trainer, you would not even consider a 300-pound fat dude with a Big Mac in each hand and no visible muscle anywhere.

You would look for a muscular dude, one that you want to look like, and ask him to show you how he got that way. You want to feel confident in the trainer. You want to know that he can help you achieve the results, and who better for the job than someone who has done it?

The first thing a good trainer would do is show you the things that you were doing that have prevented you from achieving your goals. Then he would develop a fitness program for you.

Part of your fitness program would consist of resistance training 'cause the pros know resistance builds strength and endurance.

This devotional is your spiritual personal trainer for week one. It has shown you the things that prevent you from achieving spiritual growth in the area of sexual purity.

Each time you resist the old habit of viewing porn or engaging in premarital sex, you will feel a little stronger. And you will soon find that little results produce bigger results. Small victories strung together over time equal big victories, which cause explosive spiritual growth.

James says,

> "Submit yourselves then, to God. Resist the devil, and he will flee from you."
>
> (James 4:7)

ADDITIONAL TRAINING

Grab a copy of the Bible. Look up these verses: Colossians 3:5-10, Ephesians 5 (all of it), Galatians 5:16-18.

Remember a journey of a thousand miles begins with the first step.
Get to steppin'.

Week 1 Day 6

STAY PLUGGED IN

As you focus and commit to staying pure, many things will be there to drag you down. Temptation will be in your face, even more than before.

That's how the enemy works. He does not want you to escape from your old life. Your friends may not understand your new desire to avoid sexual content or having sex. They'll probably bust on you and try to make you feel like you're the one doing wrong.

It will be important to find a mentor, someone you trust to talk to when times get tough or when you are tempted to give in.

Just like a cordless drill that runs low and needs to be recharged, you will feel drained at times. We've all had those moments and at times still do. That's why you need to stay plugged in to God's word. That's why you need to find some like-minded people to walk this out with.

DRINK IT IN

This week we talked about building muscle as being a scientific process. Part of the process of muscle development is water. The more water you drink the bigger your muscles will get. Water intake into your muscles gives you that pumped look. You feel better and stronger when you drink water instead of soda.

The same process is true in spiritual development. The more of God's word you drink in, the stronger you grow in faith and your resistance against temptation becomes greater.

DON'T COMPROMISE

Choosing to follow God's will for your life is not always easy, but He never leaves you.

Find the book of Daniel in the Old Testament and read chapter six. Yes, all of it. It's not that long.

You'll see that Daniel did not compromise and God honored him. If you make the commitment to stay pure, you can be confident that you are not alone in this. There are many others just like you.

Tomorrow in your devotional a teen will tell his story of porn addiction and how he overcame the struggles. I hope you are encouraged and choose to honor God and your future wife by remaining pure.

Visit our Facebook group page, REGENER8, and tell your story.

Teen Take

Always hungry, never satisfied.

Always thirsty, never satisfied.

Always want more, never satisfied.

Some doors are better left unopened. Unfortunately, we tend to ignore the "Do Not Enter" sign and enter anyway. Such was my case several years ago. I figured that one look wouldn't hurt. It would just satisfy my curiosity. I had no idea what was in the Pandora's box I was about to open.

The "Enter" option illuminated the screen. Ignoring all the warnings I'd received growing up, I clicked it. Those two seconds changed my life forever, and turned me from an innocent kid into nothing short of a drug addict. The only difference between me and a crackhead is that porn is free, and I had access to it. That "one time" visit turned into hours a day. Even when I wasn't online, I was thinking about what I'd seen and what I wanted to see later.

My lust grew out of control. I couldn't get enough, and I was miserable. I hated who I was. I knew it wasn't me. I was enslaved by my addiction.

Soon the images on the screen weren't enough, and I desperately craved the real thing. I wanted to play out my fantasies for real. Luckily, I never had the opportunity to do something even more stupid than I had already done.

Your secrets will find you out.

I tried to stop, but I couldn't turn my eyes away. One week felt like an eternity, and the longest I was able to go without porn was 30 days.

Then one day it happened—I got caught.

I was ashamed, but did that stop me? No, I discreetly continued—this time I was even sneakier. I desperately tried to fulfill my lust, but no amount of porn could fill it. I was sick. I hated myself, and I contemplated suicide several times. In the whole process, I turned my back on God. I didn't want to have anything to do with church, religion, God, Jesus, any of it. I knew I was a sinner, and I knew no one loved me.

THE TRUTH WILL SET YOU FREE

I was desperate to get clean, but I couldn't tell anybody. I had become an angry, hateful, disrespectful person. I needed to change.

Then I attended a concert with some friends. One band played a song about how God loves you no matter how many stupid things you've done. I fell to my knees in the dirt and cried. I knew I was a failure, and that I needed God in my life, and that I couldn't end my addiction alone.

COLD TURKEY

There is no nicotine patch for porn. There is no reducing the amount of it in your bloodstream. The only way to stop is cold turkey. And if you've tried to stop doing anything abruptly, you know how hard it is. I was still struggling, trying to beat it by myself, and getting nowhere. "Oh one last time" was the lie I told myself over and over again.

I was at the point of giving up. Then I talked to my friend. Out of shame, I'd never told him I was a porn addict, but I knew it was time to call for outside help.

I spilled my guts. He just listened, and listened, and listened. When I was done, he gave me a hug and told me he knew I could beat this. We prayed. For the next few years he called or texted every day. Sometimes he just stopped by and asked if I was "clean."

His accountability changed the tide in my battle, and for once I finally held the high ground. I had God and my best friend in the trenches with me. It was a fight I could win!

If you're struggling with an addiction to porn, you can't win alone. You need someone to fight alongside you, someone to help you get back up when you fall, to encourage you when you don't see an end in sight. The best person you can have on your team is Jesus Christ. There's nothing you can do that will ever separate you from the love of Jesus. Don't abuse grace, either. I did that: Act all sorry so that you have peace of mind when you go to bed, but having every intention to do it all over again.

KICK PORN'S BUTT

1. Confess.

2. Accept the gift Jesus gives you—a new start.

3. Get someone you trust to be your accountability partner.

4. Read the Bible when you get the urge to look at porn.

5. Location, Location, Location—avoid situations where you will be tempted to look at porn.

6. Never quit. Always fight.

Signed,
One Who Knows

Truth About Drugs

Week 2 Day 1

TRUE OR FALSE: DOING DRUGS IS FUN

If you're the average teenager in America, you've probably heard a hundred anti-drug messages. You probably completed the D.A.R.E program at your junior high school, and were required to write a little essay on the evils of smoking pot and doing drugs.

The powers that be (adults, parents, teachers, pastors) try to convince you that the answer to the above question is false. That's a lie.

If they told you that drinking alcohol is not fun, you guessed it—that's a lie.

When I was your age, I listened to all the same messages and believed them. Drugs equal no fun. Alcohol equals no fun. Got it.

The only problem was that every beer commercial I saw had a bunch of hot babes and cool-looking dudes having a killer time, laughing, drinking, shooting pool, and smoking cigarettes. You name it.

It all looked pretty good to me. I started thinking maybe the people that told me drugs were no fun just felt that way because they never tried them. They just were misinformed. They just didn't know the people in the commercials. Or they lied to me.

These same adults would tell me great stories about these amazingly talented drug addicts. They glamorized people like Jim Belushi and Jimi Hendrix, Janis Joplin and John Bonham. When I was a teen, those stars were the equivalent of Heath Ledger and Amy Winehouse. Or Paul Gray from Slipknot.

Adults told me all about the sixties and how fun those years were: free love and drugs. LSD and Woodstock. I don't know about you, but it all sounded pretty fun to me.

I came to the conclusion that doing drugs was indeed fun and might make me creative and famous. Not a bad mix.

A LITTLE RESEARCH TEST

At the age of 16, I decided it was time to find out for myself if doing drugs was bad for me or just a lie to keep me from having fun.

I got together with some of my friends who were always high, and from the looks of things, having a good time. I told them I wanted to see what this pot thing was all about.

I smoked one joint with them, then another. Before I knew it, I was laughing and having a blast.

It was all a lie. I'd been deceived. I wasted years staying away from drugs. I missed all this fun. I was mad.

What else were they lying about? That's exactly what I was wondering.

What they should have told me was the truth: That, at first, drugs seem like fun. That, yes, I'd laugh and feel lightheaded and want to eat a bunch of Doritos®. But all good things come to an end.

YOU LOSE THAT LOVIN' FEELING

That initial high won't last, though. As the body gets used to the drugs, they won't have the same effect. In order to achieve the same high I first experienced, I'd have to move on to harder, more dangerous drugs.

But that high is fleeting as well. Axl Rose said it best in his song, "Mr. Brownstone": "I use to do a little, but a little wouldn't do, so the little got more and more."

There's a guy who knows what he's talking about.

If I'm a user, I'll constantly be chasing that first buzz. My "fun" habit will become an addiction that will control and eventually destroy my life. If anyone had told me these facts, I would've been deterred.

But instead adults chose to tell me doing drugs was no fun. I'm not gonna make the same mistake with you.

Drugs seem like fun for a while, but ask any addict if he enjoys drugs.

Remember this: If you never start, you'll never have to try to quit.

Week 2 Day 2

BLUE LIGHT SPECIAL

Have you ever owned a backyard bug BBQ? One of those cool blue neon lights that all the moths and annoying insects swarm around? The soft soothing light mesmerizes the insects into a false sense of security. It lulls them into believing there is no danger. They blindly fly into the light, only to be vaporized into crispy critters.

MONKEY SEE - MONKEY DO

Now, you'd think that after witnessing 2.3 million of their friends burst into flames, their little faces distorted in agony, that bugs would avoid the light at all costs.

But no, bugs see the carnage but convince themselves that *they* won't suffer the same fate. That somehow they'll dodge the bullet that no one else seemed able to deflect.

They can touch the pretty blue light with the soothing humming sound, and it won't hurt them. It won't have the same effect on them. They're not like all the others. Somehow they'll beat it.

YOU CAN'T FIX STUPID

As crazy as the bugs' behavior sounds, there are tens of thousands of teenagers, maybe someone you know, living life as crazy and as reckless as those clueless insects.

They see countless news stories of young people overdosing on drugs. Musicians and movie stars cut down in their prime from drugs.

They see fatal accidents due to alcohol consumption. Their friends dying before they even get to prom. But even after witnessing all these tragedies, they put the bullet in the proverbial gun, spin the chamber, and pull the trigger.

I'm at a loss to explain this self-destructive behavior. It defies logic. "Doing drugs makes me cool."

That's the real reason most people do drugs. They think they'll impress their friends, that doing drugs will make them popular.

HERE'S THE PROBLEM

That's a lie invented by Satan. The Bible calls him the Father of Lies. It's what he does. He's the best at it. It's at the top of his résumé.

The Bible says he's a roaring lion searching the whole world for people to destroy and devour. You ever see a lion rip apart its prey? That's what Satan wants to do to you.

HE'S NOT STUPID

If Satan showed you the end result of drug use, he'd have a hard time getting most people to do drugs. Yeah, there'd be a few that would still do it, but not many.

The Bible also calls Satan the Angel of Light.

WHAT THE HECK DOES THAT MEAN?

Sounds crazy to be calling Satan the Father of Lies, and a roaring lion waiting to rip you limb from limb, and then also call him an Angel of Light. Confusing? Sounds like the Bible's contradicting itself.

AT LEAST IT DOES IF YOU DON'T UNDERSTAND WHAT IT MEANS

I'll give you an example. If cigarette companies put a picture of a blackened lung that looked like a piece of charcoal on the package, would people think twice about smoking? Of course they would. Not good for business. So instead they produce ads filled with good-looking people having a great time while enjoying their products.

You buy the lie.

That's how Satan works. He doesn't advertise the bad stuff. He wraps it in a pretty package. Makes you feel all warm and fuzzy about it. That's the Angel of Light part. The Father of Lies, roaring lion part, comes later.

After you're hooked, your life's in ruins. You've lost your integrity, your friends, your family, yourself. When it's too late, then the curtain is pulled back, and you see it all for what it was.

The light was really
darkness in disguise.

Week 2 Day 3

ROTTEN APPLES = BAD PIES

I'm sure you've heard the old adage about one rotten apple spoiling the whole bunch, or bad company corrupting good morals. If you haven't, well, now you have.

Anyway, it's true, and I've experienced it first-hand on several occasions in my life.

When I was a teenager, I got myself into trouble many times, and over half of them were a direct result of the people I hung out with.

They were up to no good and I wanted to fit in, so I went along. It never ended well and usually resulted in me being arrested. I followed my "friends" right into the neon zapper and got fried every time.

MAYHEM AND MURDER

A few years back, there was a double murder featured in my local paper. Three men had killed a young couple in an upscale high-rise apartment building so they could steal drugs that were in the apartment. It was all caught on multiple security cameras, so they were captured immediately and charged with murder.

So here's the kicker in the story. One of the killers had a girlfriend who lived in the building. He convinced her that it would be a quick in-and-out job, and nobody would get hurt. The three men would give her a cut of the loot—all she had to do was let them into the building. Just open the door, that's it.

The girlfriend was charged with two counts of first-degree murder. The same as if she pulled the trigger. She got life in prison without the possibility of parole. Life for opening the door. She was 24 years old. Game over.

She should've read this advice. It was written several thousand years ago but is still relevant today. It's written as poetry, so bear with the colorful language:

> "My son, if sinners entice you, do not give into them. If they say, 'Come along with us; let's lie in wait for someone's blood, let's waylay some harmless soul; let's swallow them alive, like the grave, and whole, like those who go down to the pit; we will get all sorts of valuable things and fill our houses with plunder; throw in your lot with us, and we will share a common purse—my son, do not go along with them, do not set foot on their paths; for their feet rush into sin, they are swift to shed blood. How useless to spread a net in full view of all the birds! These men lie in wait for their own blood; they waylay only themselves! Such is the end of all who go after ill-gotten gain; it takes away the lives of those who get it."
>
> (Proverbs 1:10-19)

You never know where you'll end up once you light that first joint. 'Cause sin always takes you farther than you want to go, keeps you longer than you want to stay, and costs you far more than you want to pay.

Don't open the door.

Week 2 Day 4

THE DEVIL MADE ME DO IT

When we get busted for doing bad stuff, we blame everyone else. We don't want to take responsibility for our actions.

Grown men, on trial for killing 127 people, blame their parents and their childhood for their crimes. It's ridiculous but lawyers try anyway. It rarely works.

HERE'S WHY

James, the brother of Jesus, sums it up best:

> "But each one is tempted when, by *his* own evil desire, he is dragged away and enticed"
>
> (James 1:14, emphasis mine).

SLIPPERY SLOPE

James goes on to explain what happens when we smoke that first cigarette, drink that first beer, or smoke that first joint. It never stops there:

"Then, after desire has conceived, it gives birth to sin, and sin, when it is full-grown, gives birth to death" (James 1:15).

Remember, the devil can't make you do anything you don't want to do. He can only make suggestions. You make the choices.

YOU NEED A SHIELD

A shield can protect you from flaming arrows or, if you're Captain America, it can stop bullets. But you will probably never find yourself dodging bullets or flaming arrows.

There is a shield, though, that you can acquire to protect yourself against temptations that are guaranteed to come at you. It's called knowledge of the Bible.

> "I have hidden your word in my heart that I might not sin against you."
>
> (Psalm 119:11)

WHAT GOOD IS A GUN WITH NO BULLETS?

Having a Bible in your house and not reading it is like having a gun with no ammo. Either one is useless.

TAKE FIFTEEN

Minutes, that is, and read the Book of James. It's short, but packed with great insight.

If you study the word of God, you can use it to defeat Satan.

Week 2 Day 5

THAT'S DIFFERENT

This is probably not what you expected from a devotional about drug use, but that was my plan.

You're smart. You don't need me to tell you not to do drugs. You already know the dangers. And if you're already doing drugs, me spewing a bunch of facts about it will probably not make you quit.

NO PRESSURE

My goal is simple: honesty. No hype. No scare tactics.

It's all been done before, and it obviously doesn't work.

When I was in school, our teachers showed us a film called *Red Asphalt*. It showed gruesome scenes of car crashes involving drunk drivers, and it was meant to deter us from drinking. It didn't. We all agreed that would never happen to us. We were smarter than that. Some kids even laughed during the movie.

For the most part, it didn't prevent anything. I had friends who drank and than drove. I had friends who did drugs and than drove.

Some of those same friends suffered severe consequences. One drove drunk and hit a woman head-on, killing her instantly. He went to prison. Another friend got drunk and killed a man in a fight. He got life.

My friend Billy hit a tree while driving his four-wheeler. The crash ripped his face off. DOA. There are more.

Did it change us? No. We continued anyway. Fear does not work. Statistics don't deter.

What then?

LOVE CONQUERS ALL

That's what I found out over the last twenty years: When you know you are loved, that somebody out there really cares about you—the real you, scars and faults, sins and failures—then you don't have to hide in a drug-induced fantasy. You can face reality.

No matter how bad that reality is, you know you aren't alone. Somebody genuinely cares and loves you, not because of what you can do for them, but simply because you are you.

That knowledge literally saved my life and drastically changed me. That's what I want you to take away from this.

I know we don't know each other, but I wrote this book for you. I care about you, about your life, and want to see you become the person God created you to be.

WHY DO I CARE?

Because God cares about you. I've committed my life to God and the things he cares about, and He loves and cares deeply about you.

HOW MUCH?

> "For God so loved the world [you and me] that He gave His only son"
>
> (John 3:16).

"Greater love has no one than this, that he would lay down his life for his friends"

(John 15:13).

You don't need drugs for peace. You have the Prince of Peace.

Week 2 Day 6

JUST SAY YES

Instead of "just say no to drugs," say yes to life. Say yes to all the things you can have instead of all the things you would lose.

Yes to a great family life. (Okay, maybe not great, but at least decent.) Yes to a great education with endless possibilities. Yes to a good job or a great career. Yes to the respect of your peers. Yes to meeting a totally killer wife someday. Yes to your dream car. Yes to dream vacations. Yes to owning your own house. Yes to starting a family with that awesome wife, or at least having fun trying.

OR NONE OF THE ABOVE

If you don't say no to drugs, you'll never have or maintain the things listed above.

Drugs rob you of those things. Drugs steal your desires and ambitions. Drugs make people distrust you, avoid you, and talk bad about you.

You'll never have a good job that lasts, especially with drug testing on the rise.

No awesome woman will want you. Yeah, you may find a fellow

addict to marry who's only missing a few teeth, but hey, you'll be too stoned to care.

You get the picture? If you think I'm blowing smoke up your —-, never mind. Anyway, find some drug addicts who are older. See what they have, but more importantly, what they don't. Ask them if they're happy.

DON'T KNOW WHERE TO FIND ANY?

Check skid row. Most live there 'cause it's free. They don't have to worry about their families because they have long been written off.

They don't need electricity 'cause they don't have an alarm clock to set to get up for work because they don't have a job.

They can wear the same clothes every day 'cause they don't have anybody to impress. Lucky dogs.

Just themselves and the great outdoors 24/7. They even get to pee in an alley and don't have to shower.

Ah, the drug life.

Teen Take

Before I met Rob (Cook) and everyone who supported 252 Underground,* I was smoking weed everyday after school and on weekends. My friends and I would hang out and just chill, smoke, and have a good time. There were days that sucked: not having any money for weed, people asking to join in when there wasn't enough, or people messing with me when I was high.

I'm not saying weed is fun to do every day or at all. I'm saying it's a waste of time and money. When I first stepped in 252 Underground, I thought it was just a place to hang. I started to realize it was much more than that. It was a place to keep kids like you and me off the streets, away from drugs, fights, getting in trouble, etc.

One day when I walked in, everyone was wondering what that smell was, and I realized it was me. I got so scared that people would call the cops on me for smelling like weed since I'd smoked before I went. I literally ditched the rest of my weed down the drain and told Rob what happened. He forgave me, and I promised I'd never smoke again. Because I finally realized there was more than just smoking weed and having a good time. Weed was messing my life up: friends looking at me different, bad grades in school, and not being able to get a job.

So that's what changed it for me. Even though I don't get high off of weed anymore, I still get high off of life because I don't need weed to have a good time.

Signed,
Pete

We are very proud of Pete. He went from a pothead to an awesome young man in a transformation that was truly miraculous.

---

*Note: 252 Underground is a youth ministry my wife and I founded to reach the young people of our community and to share God's love with them. Check out *www.252underground.com* to learn more.

Truth about
the Bible

REGENER8

Week 3 Day 1

YOU WANT MUSTARD WITH THAT?

If you don't believe in God, don't worry. I'm not here to bash you with the Bible or tell you that you are going to hell. I won't tell you that you are going to heaven, either.

I am hoping that, since you are reading this, you are searching for the truth.

Welcome, oh great seeker of the truth. Now that you have found me at the top of this snow-covered mountain, I will now reveal all the secrets of the universe.

OKAY, MAYBE NOT

Maybe you have a little faith in God, but you aren't really sure what this whole Jesus thing is all about.

So you haven't walked on water, but you've gotten your feet a little wet in this Christianity thing.

HAVING JUST A LITTLE FAITH IS OKAY

Jesus said,

> "I tell you the truth, if you have faith as small as a mustard seed, you can say to this mountain, Move from

here to there and it will move. Nothing will be impossible for you"

(Matthew 17:20).

You ever see a mustard seed? If not, use a magnifying glass.

JUST THE FACTS

I'm an extremely skeptical person by nature. Just ask my wife. She'll tell you I believe none of what I hear and only half of what I see—and that's not far from the truth.

So I get it if you have trouble with the whole God and Jesus thing. I did too.

What got me thinking about the possibility that Jesus really did come back to life were His disciples.

THEY WERE YELLOW-BELLIED CHICKENS

When Jesus died and was buried, the disciples ran away. They were scared. Peter, the big tough guy, lied and said he didn't even know who Jesus was.

They all scattered and went back to their old lives. Jesus wasn't the king who was going to make everything right for the Jewish people. The disciples threw in the towel and figured they'd wait on a new savior.

BUT THEN SOMETHING HAPPENED

If you read the New Testament (that's the part of the Bible that was written after Jesus was born), you will find that these same cowards not only regrouped, but eleven of the twelve eventually died for their faith in Jesus.

I couldn't stop thinking about what made the difference. What made them come out so boldly in the name of Christ?

I put myself in their sandals. What would make *me* believe? Only one thing: seeing Jesus come back from the dead, just like he said.

A band of yellow-bellied cowards became an unstoppable force that started a movement that is still in existence today—over 2,000 years later.

THAT GOT ME THINKING

What else might be true? It started out as curiosity. I was just dipping my toe in the water. A mustard seed faith.

The more I learned, the more I became convinced that the Bible is true and everything in it happened just as it is written.

This week we are going to look at facts in the Bible that will hopefully grow your mustard seed into a tree with deep roots.

Now where did I put that hot dog?

Week 3 Day 2

IN THE BLUE TRUNKS

A popular misconception is that the Bible and science are at odds. The Bible is the 110–pound weakling, cowering in the corner, and science is the freakishly large MMA fighter waiting to destroy the credibility of the Bible with vicious blows of theory and evidence.

BUT SCIENCE IS ALL BARK, NO BITE

The science freak may run around the cage making a scene, screaming equations and getting the crowd all riled up. Problem is, that's all he's got. Nothing more than a Chihuahua in pit bull clothing.

Public education lays out the theory of evolution like it's factual. And it implies that the Bible's on the ropes, ready to tap out.

Many dismiss the Bible, arguing that science disproves it, but that's because they've never read it.

ONCE UPON A TIME...

You might've heard the Bible described as nothing more than fairy tales and myths. Only fools believe what's written in its pages.

"Experts" (and, yes, my voice is dripping with sarcasm) claim that the Bible is rooted in science fiction, not science fact.

Let me punch a few holes in their "theory."

If you have a copy of the Bible lying around, let's check out Leviticus. (Not a popular baby name now, let me tell you.)

Anyway, Leviticus is the third book of the Bible, so it's way in the front. It was written in 1400 B.C. (when your parents were just kids).

Leviticus 17:11a says,

"For the life of the flesh is in the blood."

Blood is necessary for survival, just ask Dracula. If you don't believe me, try living without it.

Sounds crazy right? Well, prior to 1616 A.D., if you were sick, doctors would probably have drained your blood to heal you. They thought that blood in your body is what made you sick. Their quick fix? Get rid of it.

You can probably guess the outcome even if you are not a doctor or a rocket scientist. DOA.

OOPS

Then along comes William Harvey in 1616 (Google him later), and he actually has a clue. He discovers that blood circulation is necessary for life. (Tell him what he won, Johnny.)

What gave it away? All the dead people without blood? I'd have figured that out after the thirtieth or fortieth dead dude, but I'm a slow learner.

Thus—drum roll please—William "the brain" Harvey confirmed what the Bible had revealed 3,000 years earlier.

So the next time you're out skateboarding, and you attach your face to the pavement and see all that blood, think of the Bible as fact.

Week 3 Day 3

JURASSIC FARCE

Another popular argument among the anti-Bible crowd is the Bible's failure to mention dinosaurs.

How come the Bible doesn't mention dinosaurs? The answer is really simple: ignorance.

Oh wait, you thought I meant the Bible. Sorry, I meant the people who claim the Bible does not mention dinosaurs make that statement out of ignorance.

They would have to change their belief if they actually read the Bible.

Let's play archeologists. Go dig up your Bible.

You won't find dinosaurs in the Bible for a very good reason: the term *dinosaur* was not coined until 1841 A.D. The Bible called them *tanniyn*. *Tanniyn* are mentioned twenty-eight times in the Bible.

Different species of dinosaurs were known by different names. In the book of Job (chapter 40 verses 15 to 24) God describes the behemoth. Since 1930, behemoth has been known as Brachiosaurus.

In Job 40:1-34, you can read the description of the leviathan. Since 1901, it has been known as Kronosaurus.

Take a few minutes and read those verses.

When you have all the facts, you can make an informed decision about the accuracy of the Bible.

Next time some old fossil tries to tell you the Bible doesn't mention dinosaurs you can set them straight.

Week 3 Day 4

LIKE A SIEVE

Well, it's day four, and we've managed to punch some pretty large holes in some of the most popular arguments made by the "experts" as to the legitimacy of the Bible. But we have a whole week, so why stop now?

Ah, Mother Earth—that big, beautiful marble floating in space. It almost feels like home.

You really can't argue with that sentence because you know the earth is round and floating in space. At least you know that today.

But that was not always the case among the so-called experts.

Just a few hundred years ago, the popular theory was the earth was flat. Flat as a pancake.

There is even a group in existence today called the Flat Earth Society that still believes that, although I'm not quite sure why. (Google® them.)

THE BIBLE'S TAKE

In **600 B.C.**, the prophet Isaiah wrote:

> "It is He who sits above the circle of the earth."
>
> (Isaiah 40:22 NIV)

Hindus, Greeks, and Buddhists believed the earth was held up by a number of things: a man, an elephant, a catfish, or some other physical support.

THE BIBLE'S TAKE

"He spreads out the northern skies over empty space; he suspends the earth over nothing"

(Job 27:1 NIV)

That was written 2,800 years before the discovery of gravity.

AHEAD OF ITS TIME

The Bible went against all logic and knowledge at the time of its writing, and it still does today.

Think about that for a hot minute 'cause tomorrow's devo will be in your face—and probably in a couple other uncomfortable places.

Next time someone tells you
the Bible is a fairy tale, you can
tell him that's *flat* out ridiculous.

Week 3 Day 5

MYTHBUSTERS

We've spent the last week re-discovering the accuracy of the Bible. We've also debunked the "science trumps the Bible" myth.

TAP OUT DENIED

Science does not have a choke-hold on the Bible. The Word of God is not down for the count.

As we discussed yesterday, the Bible defied the logic of its day and was, in fact, ahead of its time.

SO WHAT?

You may feel indifferent to learning the Bible is true and accurate. Maybe you don't care that the statements made in the Bible, thousands of years ago, have been verified through modern science.

So you won't be starting a "The Bible Is Real" fan page on Facebook® or tweeting Bible verses to your friends. I get it, that's cool. They'd probably only call you a freak anyway. That won't adversely affect you.

BUT THIS WILL

> "Therefore the Lord himself will give you a sign: The virgin will be with child and will give birth to a son, and will call him Immanuel."
>
> (Isaiah 7:14 NIV)

Sounds like the Christmas story, right? Here's the kicker: It was written 740 years before Jesus was born.

Imagine if you found an article written 740 years before you were born that described your birth. OMG!

Some skeptics might try to dismiss that verse in Isaiah as a fluke, and that might fly if that's all there was to the story, but…

THERE'S MORE

Grab your Bible and find Isaiah 53:1-12. It is a biographical piece about the life, death, and resurrection of Jesus Christ.

It's extremely brief but amazingly accurate. If it had been written after Jesus died, it would've made a nice eulogy in the *Jerusalem Gazette*.

But, as you probably guessed, it was also written 740 plus years before Jesus was born.

If you add up all the evidence, you can only come to one conclusion: The Bible is true and factually accurate.

Jesus was born, he lived, and he died on a Roman cross. The Bible states that Jesus is the only way to heaven.

ASK YOURSELF…

If everything else in the Bible is true, what does this mean for me?

What will you do with this knowledge?

ABC

The Bible says we need to **A**dmit that we messed up. We need to **B**elieve in Jesus. And we need to **C**onfess our sins and ask God for forgiveness.

If you do that, all your screw-ups will be erased: the record is clean, white as fresh, fallen snow.

FRESH START

The Bible says old things are gone; all things are new. It's the ultimate pardon. And it's free.

What are you waiting for?

Week 3 Day 6

BY FAITH

> "And without faith it is impossible to please God, because anyone who comes to him must believe that he exists and that he rewards those who earnestly seek him."
>
> (Hebrews 11:6 NIV)

> It all starts with faith, and the Bible's definition of faith is this: "Now faith is being sure of what we hope for and certain of what we do not see."
>
> (Hebrews 11:1 NIV)

You can be sure that what God has promised is true. He has proven Himself throughout the pages of the Bible. He has proven Himself through science, and He has proven that He loves you and wants to have a relationship with you by sending His son, Jesus, to die on the cross in your place.

Jesus took our punishment, the punishment you and I deserved. He stepped up and we were pardoned.

SEE FOR YOURSELF

You don't need to take my word for it. You don't know me. I'm just some dude who wrote a book.

Investigate. Read the Bible for yourself. You will find the same things I found, and hopefully your faith will grow from a mustard seed.

STEROID BOOST

For those of you reading this book that already had a little faith, hopefully your faith was strengthened this week. I showed you evidence that the Bible is accurate and reliable, but there is so much more, too much in fact, to list here. You too can explore the Bible for yourself and see what you can uncover.

FAITH WORKS

What do you do with this new-found faith?

James the brother of Jesus asks an important question:

> **"What good is it, my brothers, if a man claims to have faith but has no deeds? Can such faith save him?"**
>
> (James 2:14)

When I first read that verse, I was confused because I had read in the Book of Ephesians, written by the Apostle Paul, something that seemed to contradict James' line of thinking:

> **"For it is by grace you have been saved, through faith—and this not of yourselves, it is a gift of God—not by works, so that no man can boast."**
>
> (Ephesians 2:9 NIV)

You see my dilemma? And if that wasn't enough to confuse me, James took it even further:

> "But some will say, 'You have faith; I have deeds.' Show me your faith without deeds, and I will show you my faith by what I do'"
>
> (James 2:26 NIV)

CLEAR AS MUD

One dude says I'm saved through faith, not works. The other dude says faith without works won't save me. It seemed like a catch-22. I could not win, so why bother trying? At least that's how I felt before I became a firefighter.

HEAD KNOWLEDGE

When I joined the fire department, I was required to take about 300 hours of training and multiple tests. I even had to study a 400-page fire-fighting manual.

I completed all of my training and passed all my tests. I was now a certified firefighter. They gave me a pager that would go off in the event of a fire, and it went off quite often. I went to every fire call without fail. I was a firefighter.

But what if, after all those hours of training and all those tests were completed, I never went on one fire call? What if, when the pager went off, I just turned it off and continued doing whatever it was I was doing?

What if I never put out a fire? What if I only rode on the fire truck when there was a parade? Would you consider me a firefighter? Would *anyone* consider me a firefighter?

To be a firefighter, you actually have to put out fires. That's how it works.

MAKES SENSE

When I thought about what James was saying, it clicked: faith only works with action. If I say I believe it, I should live it. That's how it works. Just like if I say I love my wife, there will be actions to back it up, evidence of my love.

So Paul says you can't do anything to earn salvation, and James says once you are saved, there will be evidence of it in your life.

Don't talk about it.
Be about it.

The more you walk it, the less you have to talk it. They say actions speak louder than words.

Let your life scream.

Teen Take

When Rob told me about the topic this week and asked if I could write something, I started thinking about one of the instances that helped me believe that the Bible was true. Oddly enough, the story of Christopher Columbus did it.

The whole country mocked and ridiculed Columbus for saying he could sail east by going west. At that time the world was "known" to be flat. What would compel Columbus to embark on such a ludicrous venture? The decision to set sail when everyone around him assured him it would end in death was a great leap of faith.

Did Christopher Columbus know something they didn't know? In faith he left Europe and traveled west in order to go east. Guess what? He made it! Well, he found land and didn't fall off the edge of the world, at least. He didn't find India; instead he found America. I'm still amazed that he stuck to his guns and did what they said couldn't be done. He proved all the "scientists" of that era wrong.

Guess what? The world is round.

Signed,
Byron H.

Truth About Religion

Week 4 Day 1

RULES? WE DON'T NEED NO STINKIN' RULES

Do not touch. Do not enter. No Skate boarding. No trespassing. No loitering. No shoes, no shirt, no service.

When I was a teenager, I hated rules. It seemed to me that rules were meant to keep me from having fun.

To be completely honest, I just didn't want anyone telling me what to do. Usually when someone told me not to do something, it made me want to do it more.

I'm no longer a teenager but, to tell you the truth, I still don't like rules.

My wife calls me a rebel. I can't say I disagree. I question everything. I want to know the reason behind why I can't do something. And "just because" never seems to satisfy me.

IT'S NOT ABOUT RULES

When I heard about God and Jesus, the first thing that popped into my mind was that list of ten rules. You know, the Ten Commandments.

I knew the kind of person I was, and I knew I'd have trouble following some list of do's and don'ts. It would be a constant struggle for me to please God.

Fortunately, somebody told me a story. Here's the story in my own words.

Jesus and His disciples are out there busting their butts, sharing the Gospel, feeding hungry people by the thousands, and healing people—all kinds of crazy stuff. Jesus is raising people from the dead. You catch that? *From the dead.* So, in the middle of all this insanity, the disciples are walking through a wheat field, and they're picking the grain and eating it, 'cause they're hungry. Along come the religious leaders, and they gather around Jesus and his posse.

A PAT ON THE BACK

Were they there to congratulate them for all their hard work and sacrifice? Were they there to encourage them? Offer assistance? Heck no. They criticized the disciples for not washing their hands before eating the grain, 'cause apparently that was their custom, one of the religious leaders' rules.

Bad move one their part, 'cause Jesus opens a case of verbal beat-down.

CHECK THIS OUT

Jesus tells them:

> "Who cares if your hands are clean when your heart is filthy? You look good outside by what you say, but you don't do it."
>
> (Matthew 23:27-28)

IT'S ABOUT RELATIONSHIP

Imagine that my wife gave me a list of rules that went something like this:

Don't cheat on me.

Buy me flowers once a week.

Take me out to dinner once a week.

Put the toilet seat down.

Never eat the last fudge brownie.

Wash my car every Saturday.

Tell me I'm beautiful every day.

Etc., etc., etc.

What kind of relationship do you think we'd have? How do you think I'd feel about my wife? How would my wife know if I really loved her or if was just following the rules?

My wife doesn't need to give me a list of rules on how to treat her. I know how to treat my wife because I love her. I do special things for her because I want to surprise her and make her smile. You get it?

I don't need anyone telling me not to cheat on my wife. I don't cheat on my wife because I love my wife. Does that make sense? Hopefully, you said yes.

That's the kind of relationship Jesus is looking for with you. He knows that if you love Him, He's not going to have to give you a big list of rules to follow. It will come naturally to you.

When I work with teens, I never talk about rules. My job is to show them how much Jesus loves them and help them fall in love with Jesus.

If I can accomplish that, I'm not gonna have to run around behind them telling them what they should and should not do.

This week I want to share with you the kind of relationship Jesus wants with you.

My hope is that you fall in love with Him.

Week 4 Day 2

NO HOOPS

Jesus doesn't set up an obstacle course with hoops to jump through in order to be in a relationship with Him.

He doesn't have a list of requirements that you must fulfill so He can check them all off.

That's religion. That's man trying to reach God and putting conditions on it.

Jesus doesn't care what color your hair is. He doesn't care if you have a Mohawk. So what if your lip is pierced?

Jesus isn't looking at all that. He's looking at your heart.

NO ONE IS DISQUALIFIED

Unlike amusement parks, there's no sign in front of heaven that says you must be this tall to enter.

This is what Jesus says to you:

> "Come to me, *all* you who are weary and burdened, and I will give you rest. Take my yoke upon you and learn from me, for I am gentle and humble in heart, and you will find rest for your souls. For my yoke is

easy and my burden is light."

(Matthew 11:28-30 NIV, emphasis mine)

SO CUT OUT THE MIDDLEMAN

Religious leaders want to weigh you down with a bunch of rules and regulations. They want you to fulfill their requirements before they allow you to come to Jesus.

Jesus was not too keen on them back in His day. He still isn't. You don't need a middleman to reach Jesus. You can go right to Him personally.

You don't even need to download the iJesus app.

Week 4 Day 3

THE METHOD TO THE MADNESS

So why would Jesus leave heaven and come down here, just to be mocked and killed?

I've often wondered why He did. What motivated Jesus the King to leave His kingdom and come to earth as a helpless baby? Why did He volunteer to go through puberty, become a homeless servant, and die a horrible death on a cross after being betrayed by a close friend?

I know I don't have what it takes to do that. But here's the reason Jesus gives us for going through all that He did. His own words recorded in the Book of Matthew:

> "For I have come from heaven not to do my will but the will of him who sent me. And this is the will of him who sent me, that I shall lose none of all that he has given me, but raise them up at the last day. For my Father's will is that everyone who looks to the Son and believes in him shall have eternal life, and I will raise him up at the last day."
>
> (John 6:38-40 NIV)

FOR YOU

Jesus did it for you and for me. He gave His life for us. He loves us (yes, you too), no matter what you've done.

Jesus gave up paradise for poverty, kingship for servant-hood, royalty for a crown of thorns, so that he could take our punishment that we rightly deserve. He provided a pardon through His sacrifice.

That should prove His love to you. Who do you know that would do all of that for you?

Not one person on my Facebook® friends' list would even consider it. I'm certain the same goes for you.

LOVE SONG

Bruno Mars might claim that he would take a grenade for you, but that's only a song, nothing more.

I LOVE YOU MORE

If you have a girlfriend, you've probably said, "I love you," even if you didn't mean it. Then she says, "I love you more." Then you say, "I love you more." Then she counters with a little giggle and says (you guessed it), "I love you more." That whole episode goes on for—gag me with a spoon—umpteen minutes, and is repeated on a daily basis. At least until one of you decide that he/she suddenly loves someone else more.

That's why it's so hard for us to understand what true love is. We equate love with good feelings. As long as we feel good, we are in love. If our significant other is treating us great, we are in love. Not so great, bye-bye love. Next.

To really understand love, you have to see it through the eyes of Jesus.

Jesus loves us even when we don't love Him. He chose the cross knowing that humanity would mock and ridicule Him. That we would rather sleep in on Sunday.

That we would rather not think about Him because thinking about Him might mean we shouldn't do some of the things we do. And that would ruin our fun.

None of this deterred Jesus from loving you.

The Bible is a love story, and we are the objects of Jesus' affection.

Next time someone says he'd die for you, say, "Thanks, but somebody already beat you to it."

Week 4 Day 4

SHOW ME THE LOVE

So we've established that Jesus loves you and me. And He gave His life to prove it. But it doesn't end there. In fact, that's really only the beginning.

Jesus wants to be a part of your everyday life. He wants you to talk to Him. Tell Him your fears and troubles, your victories and challenges.

When I was first starting to go to church and hanging out with "church people," they use to say some crazy stuff. At least I thought it was crazy at the time.

INSANE IN THE BRAIN

That's not to say I don't hear ridiculous stuff nowadays, but there's a big difference between crazy and ridiculous, trust me.

One of the things I found crazy was someone saying, "God told me this" or "God told me that."

WHERE'S THE STAIGHT JACKET?

I was like, "Are you nuts?" (Well, at least that's what I said in my head.) Anyway, I couldn't understand nor did I believe God was talking to people, let alone telling them what to do. It was utter nonsense to me.

He may have talked to people in Bible times. But that was then, this is now. We are sophisticated. We don't wear robes and sandals.

VOICES IN THEIR HEAD?

I'd ask them, "Really? God spoke to you?" They'd assure me that He had. I was like, "Wow, that's cool." All the while, I was looking for an escape.

They obviously saw the distress in my face, and then they'd feel the need to explain. It went something like this: "I don't actually here God's voice audibly..." That made me feel a little better until they finished the sentence: "...I hear Him in my head." Coo Coo.

What did he just say? He hears voices in his head. And he looked so normal. You just never can tell.

This scenario played out many times. I just learned to smile and nod and insert a "wow" or "that's cool" here and there.

All that changed one day when God spoke to me. And God being God and all decided that I needed to be taught a lesson.

He chose to speak to me in an audible voice. There's not enough room here for the story behind it, but I'd be lying if I said that I did not freak out.

He only spoke to me once in an audible voice, but it was enough to make a believer out of me. I'm sure you might think that I'm crazy or that I imagined it.

I'm okay with that, because someday God may prove otherwise.

Since then, I've heard the voice of God many times, but it'd be more accurate to say I hear it in my spirit rather than in my head.

I started to look for an explanation in the Bible. This is what I found:

"My sheep listen to my voice; I know them, and they follow me."

(John 10:27 NIV)

Let me give you one example of an instance when I heard God speak to me and how it played out.

I was driving to work, and I heard God in my spirit. He told me to buy groceries for a family that I hadn't seen in quite a while. I turned around and went home. I got my wife, and we went shopping for the family. When we delivered the food, the woman started crying. She said she'd just prayed that morning and asked God to provide food for her family. Her husband had hurt his back and was out of work. When we helped put the groceries away, we saw that the cabinets were bare.

I can't explain what happened. Not with human reasoning.

I had no idea the family was in need, and if I hadn't "heard" God, I wouldn't have done what I did.

God wants to communicate with you. If you study His word, you will learn to recognize His voice. You will hear it, and it will always be confirmed.

*Communication is key
to any great relationship.*

Week 4 Day 5

So many young people ask me this question: "What do I have to do if I'm a Christian?"

They want to know what's the least amount they can do and still go to heaven. That's the wrong question. Being a Christian, a.k.a "follower of Christ," is not about what you *have* to do.

The real question is, "What *can* I do for Jesus?"

WHERE'S THE LINE?

Others ask me what they'll have to give up. They want to know how much of their old life they can hold on to and still "live for God."

Once again, it's the wrong attitude. We shouldn't be asking how much sinning we can do, 'cause let's face it, that's the real issue.

Our attitude should be, "How close can I get to Christ? How deep can I go in my relationship with Jesus? How far can I go in my walk with God?"

IMAGINE

If I asked my wife, "What's the least amount I can do in our relationship to prove my love to you?" or "Sweetheart, how much of my old single life can I maintain during our marriage?" What do you think she would do?

What if I said, "You know, honey, I use to date girls four nights a week, but I'd be willing to cut that down to two nights a week, and I won't do any more than kissing and touching. Is that cool?"

I'd better be quick on my feet, because she would kick my butt. She'd ask why I even bothered to marry her in the first place.

VALID QUESTION

Obviously that sounds ridiculous. But for some reason, we don't think it sounds crazy when it comes to our relationship with Jesus.

Here's Jesus in His own words:

> **"No one can serve two masters. Either you will hate the one and love the other, or you will be devoted to the one and despise the other."**
>
> (Matthew 6:24)

GIVE IT UP

When I married my beautiful wife, I forgot all about my old bachelor days. I was and still am so in love with my wife, Stephanie, that I couldn't imagine doing anything to hurt her.

I could care less about all the other girls that were in my life prior to her. I want to be hanging out with my wife instead of going out with the guys.

When I'm not with my wife, I'm thinking about her. I plan ways to make her smile. I want her to know how much I love her and care about her.

All my words wouldn't mean anything if I went out with other girls and did things with them that I should only be doing with my wife. Get it?

My wife knows I love her because I am intentional about letting her know. I don't ever think about what I gave up to be with her, and I never wonder what is the least I can get away with so she'll stay with me.

TRUE LOVE

I'm devoted to my wife. I love her. And that's exactly the kind of relationship Jesus wants with you.

Don't get spiritually married to Jesus and then stay emotionally attached to the world. That's called an affair.

CHEW ON THIS

"Do not love the world or anything in the world. If anyone loves the world, love for the Father is not in them. For everything in the world-lust of the flesh, lust of the eyes, and the pride of life-comes not from the Father but from the world. The world and its desires pass away, but whoever does the will of God lives forever."

(1 John 2:15-17 NIV)

SIDE NOTE

That doesn't mean you can't love your mommy or daddy or the pretty blue sky. The term "world" in these verses is referring to sinful things. Are we cool? Good.

Start asking the right questions.

Week 4 Day 6

SOUND ADVICE

So yesterday we established that I'm crazy about my wife, Stephanie, and that because I care about her, I care about the things she cares about.

If something is important to her, you guessed it, it becomes important to me. (Remember this stuff, guys, 'cause you'll probably be married someday, and this advice is worth the price of the book alone.)

If we are to have a great relationship with Jesus, we ought to find out what He cares about, right?

SO WHAT DOES JESUS CARE ABOUT?

The best place to research what Jesus cares about is the Bible itself.

James, the brother of Jesus, writes:

> "Religion that God our Father accepts as pure and faultless is this: to look after orphans and widows in their distress and to keep oneself from being polluted by the world."
>
> (James 1:27 NIV)

Notice that he doesn't say you have to wear a suit and uncomfortable dress shoes. He also didn't say anything about sending all your money to TV preachers.

> "But when you give a banquet, invite the poor, the crippled, the lame, the blind, and you will be blessed. Although they cannot repay you, you will be repaid at the resurrection of the righteous."
>
> (Luke 14:13-14 NIV)

PARTY TIME!

From these verses we learn that Jesus cares for the underdog. He wants us to care for the less fortunate. Orphans and widows and the poor as well as handicapped people.

We also learn that, for what we do for people in this life, God will pay us for eternity. Talk about a great investment.

BOTTOM LINE

Jesus cares about broken, hurting people. That covers all of us, because we are all broken and hurting, regardless of the façade we put up.

REMEMBER THE GOLDEN RULE

No, it's not "he who has the gold makes the rules." Jesus commanded us to do unto others as we would have done to us.

He also said to love your neighbor as you love yourself. And to love and pray for our enemies, even the people who persecute us.

WHY?

If we treat people with love regardless of what they say or do to us, we may have a chance to lead them to Christ because He died for them too. And if not, we will still be rewarded by God in the end. That's a win-win

Start storing up treasure in heaven. That's what Jesus cares about.

Additional Reading: Luke 6:30-36

Teen Take

I've done so many bad things that I never believed God could love me. I had friends that went to church, and a couple times I went with them, but I always felt like the black sheep. I could tell by the way people looked at me that I didn't belong there.

I knew there was so much stuff I had to do to make God love me; at least that's the way everybody made it seem. I'd heard of the Ten Commandments, and I knew I couldn't keep them all. I looked at girls. I smoked. I stole stuff—not all the time, though. I figured why bother? God wouldn't let me in heaven, and probably couldn't wait to send me to hell.

Things have changed over the last couple of years, though. My friends told me about this cool place they went called 252 Underground. They gave away food and candy bars and stuff. Everybody that volunteered there treated me really nice. I started going every time it was open. The people there made me feel good about myself, and they cared about me. They listened to my problems and never judged me. I started to listen to the messages on Wednesday night, and they talked about how God loved me no matter what I had done. I started to believe it, 'cause these guys from 252 loved me know matter what I did. They told me that God knows I'm not perfect—that's why He sent Jesus to pay for all the stuff I did wrong. They told me that Jesus wants a relationship with me even when I screw up.

I still struggle with stuff, but I know God loves me and wants to be involved in my life. It's cool.

Truth about Regener8tion

REGENER8

Week 5 Day 1

TRANSFORMERS

You've probably seen the mega hit movie *Transformers* or, at the very least, you've heard about it: ordinary-looking cars and trucks with the ability to transform into robots.

Those robots look nothing like their original form.

They perform extraordinary feats in their transformed state. They battle the evil Decepticons. (With a name like that, what did you expect?) The movie ends with the Autobots, (that's the good guys), victorious.

That may be just Hollywood movie magic, but God created you to be transformed, and that's not science fiction.

> "Do not conform any longer to the pattern of this world, but be transformed by the renewing of your mind."
>
> (Romans 12:2 NIV)

Okay, you don't get to turn into a flying missile-shooting robot, but hey, you can still dream.

WHAT YOU DO GET IS A BRAIN TRANSPLANT

How do you transform your mind? You may have heard this saying: "Garbage in, garbage out."

There's no shortage of garbage out there for you to consume. Hollywood is filled with violence. The Internet is overrun with pornography. And, sadly, schools are filled with drugs. How can you escape the garbage?

YOU FEEL TRAPPED

You are assaulted with violence every time you turn on the TV. Friends pressure you to do things you shouldn't. Companies market profanity-laced music and t-shirts to you.

It's not easy to do the right thing. If it was, more people would be doing it. But if you desire to please God, you'll be happy to know that when you are tempted, God always provides a way out.

> "No temptation has over taken you except what is common to mankind. And God is faithful; he will not let you be tempted beyond what you can bear. But when you are tempted, he will also provide a way out so that you can endure it."
>
> (1 Corinthians 10:13 NIV)

TOO GOOD TO BE TRUE?

That's what you may be thinking about God's promise to provide an out. But it is possible. The real problem is that we don't necessarily want a way out, or we don't try hard enough to avoid sin. That's God's take on it.

"In your struggle against sin, you have not yet resisted
to the point of shedding your blood."

(Hebrews 12:4)

Basically, God is saying we're too quick to give up without a fight.
This week I am going to show you how to overcome temptation.

This week you will put on the UFC gloves and kick the crap out of temptation.

Additional reading: Colossians 3: 5-17

Week 5 Day 2

STAY HEART HEALTHY

> "I have hidden your word in my heart, that I might not
> sin against you."
>
> (Psalm 119:11 NIV)

The most effective tool I've found for combating temptation is the Bible.

The more I read the Bible, the less I want to sin. The closer I am to God, the stronger my resistance.

Unfortunately, the less I read my Bible, the more I find myself caught up in sin.

JUST FIFTEEN MINUTES A DAY KEEPS THE DEVIL AWAY

I love to read the Bible an hour or more a day, but I know that, as a teenager, you have lots of demands on your time, so I'm suggesting that you read a minimum of fifteen minutes a day.

I also suggest you pray at least fifteen minutes a day as well. That's only a half-hour out of a 24-hour day.

Sound hard?

BREAK IT UP

You could read seven minutes in the morning and eight minutes at night. Pray while you're on the john. You can take care of business while you're taking care of business.

There's no end to the possibilities. It just takes a little effort, and the rewards far outweigh anything you'll give up.

> "Since then, you have been raised with Christ, set your hearts on things above, where Christ is seated at the right hand of God. Set your minds on things above, not on earthly things. For you died*, and your life is now hidden with Christ in God. When Christ, who is your life, appears, then you also will appear with him in glory."
>
> (Colossians 3:1-4 NIV)

(*Note: This is not talking about a physical death as in you checking out, taking a dirt nap, donating your body as worm food. This is talking about your sinful nature, the old you, as in before Jesus. Just figured I'd clarify that.)

Week 5 Day 3

PICK A PARTNER

Batman had Robin. The Lone Ranger had Tonto. Beavis had Butthead. Sherlock had Holmes—wait a minute—never mind. You get the point. Everyone needs someone he can count on. This goes all the way back to Bible times.

> "After this the Lord appointed seventy-two others and sent them two by two ahead of him to every town and place where he was about to go."
>
> (Luke 10:1 NIV)

SMARTY PANTS

King Solomon was the smartest dude who ever lived, and this is his take on the subject:

> "Two are better than one, because they have a good return on their work: If one falls down, his friend can help him up [that's kind of a no brainer], but pity the man who falls and has no one to pick him up! Also if two lie down together, they will keep warm. But how can one keep warm? Though one may be overpowered,

two can defend themselves. A cord of three strands is not quickly broken."

(Ecclesiastes 4:9-12 NIV)

Go pick up a stick and break it. Easy, right? Now pick up three together and try to break them. Get the picture?

ACCOUNTABILITY IS KEY

Find someone you can trust, and who is mature in Christ (someone who's known Him for a few years). Meet with that person at least once a week. Share your progress as well as your failures. God uses people who fail 'cause there aren't any other kinds around.

Call that person when you are faced with temptation. Ask him/her to pray for you daily.

Get around like-minded people who might be facing the same struggles. Support each other.

Life's better together.

Additional reading: Galatians 6:1-2

Week 5 Day 4

THE EPIC CONFLICT

The Apostle Paul tells us how to overcome temptation:

> "So I say live by the Spirit [the Holy Spirit, God in Spirit form], and you will not gratify the desires of the sinful nature. For the sinful nature desires what is contrary to the Spirit, and the Spirit what is contrary to the sinful nature, they are in conflict with each other, so that you do not do what you want. But if you are led by the Spirit, you are not under law."
>
> (Galatians 5:16-18 NIV)

NO LAW?

So what's with this "you are not under the law" stuff? Don't we have to obey the law?

Let me explain. The law tells me not to beat my wife. The law tells me not to murder my wife. It also tells me not to cheat on my wife.

If I love my wife—and I do—I'm not even going to consider doing anything to hurt her. Therefore, love trumps the law. I'm not under the law. The law is made for lawbreakers. If you are in Christ, you're not under the law.

PAUL EXPLAINS

> "In the same way, count yourselves dead to sin but alive to God in Christ Jesus. Therefore do not let sin reign in your mortal body so that you obey its evil desires. Do not offer parts of your body to sin, as instruments of wickedness, but rather offer yourselves to God, as those who have been brought from death to life; and offer the parts of your body to him as instruments of righteousness. For sin shall not be your master, because you are not under law, but under grace."
>
> (Romans 6:11-14 NIV)

IN A NUTSHELL

If you are busy living for God, you won't have time to sin. If you are in love with God, you won't want to sin. If you do make a mistake, you are forgiven, and that is grace.

GRACE VS. MERCY

Grace is God giving you something you *don't* deserve. Mercy is God withholding what you *do* deserve.

ALL YOU NEED IS LOVE

On one occasion, an expert in the law stood up to test Jesus.

> "Teacher," he asked, "what must I do to inherit eternal life?"

> "What's written in the Law?" Jesus responded. "How

do you read it?"

The lawyer answered, "Love the Lord your God with all your heart and with all your soul and with all your strength and with all your mind and love your neighbor as yourself."

"You have answered correctly," Jesus said. "Do this and you will live."

(Luke 10:25-28 NIV)

APOSTLE PETER'S TAKE

"Above all, love each other deeply, because love covers a multitude of sins."

(1 Peter 4:8 NIV)

WHAT'S THE BOTTOM LINE?

If you are filled with love for God and others, you're not going to be doing evil, sinful things.

> ### Live by the Holy Spirit, and let Him guide you. If you do this daily, you will overcome temptation.

Additional reading: 1 Corinthians 13:1-13

Week 5 Day 5

OPEN BOOK TEST

Peter gives us the secret to conquering temptation:

> "His [God's] divine power has given us everything we
> need for life and godliness through our knowledge of
> him who called us by his own glory and goodness.
> Through these he has given us his very great and pre-
> cious promises, so that through them you may partici-
> pate in the divine nature and escape the corruption in
> the world caused by evil desires."
>
> (2 Peter 1:3-4 NIV)

GREAT NEWS

When we ask Christ to forgive us, and we put our faith and trust in
Him alone, He gives us everything immediately. He doesn't hold anything back. We get His Spirit, who gives us the power to overcome.

ADD FIRE POWER

> "For this very reason, make every effort to add to your
> faith goodness, and to goodness, knowledge, and to

knowledge, self-control, and to self-control, perseverance, and to perseverance, godliness, and to godliness,
brotherly kindness, and to brotherly kindness, love. For
if you possess these qualities in increasing measure, they
will keep you from being ineffective and unproductive
in your knowledge of our Lord Jesus Christ."

(2 Peter 1:5-8 NIV)

It just so happens that the qualities that Peter lists are the qualities
of the Holy Spirit (they're also called the fruit of the Spirit), who
lives in you when you put your faith in Christ.

Did you ever see *Karate Kid*?

If you saw the movie with Jackie Chan and Jaden Smith, then
you saw Jackie's character put Jaden's through rigorous repetitive
training. Jaden's character thought it was pointless, but he found
out he was learning discipline and technique, which enabled him
to defeat the enemy.

The same is true when we study the Bible daily and become a
student of the Word. You may not see immediate results overnight,
but in time you will build up knowledge and character that will
enable you to defeat temptation and the devil.

Take your coat off. Now drop it.
Now pick it up. Put it on. Take it off.
Now you get the picture?

Additional reading: Galatians 5:22-26

Week 5 Day 6

ABSTINENCE = NO DIRTY DIAPERS

If you don't have sex, you won't get diseases and you won't get a girl pregnant. Now that's nothing you didn't already know, but I'm making a point, so humor me.

Just as abstinence prevents problems, overcoming temptation works the same way.

DON'T GO TO THE PARTY

Don't wait until you get to the wild party to try and figure out how you are going to resist peer pressure to drink and do drugs. Don't go to the party in the first place. If I were a recovering alcoholic, I wouldn't apply for a job as a bartender. If I am a recovering porn addict, I don't apply for a job as a bouncer at a topless dance club.

I don't put myself in situations where I might be tempted to drink or view porn. Get it?

Don't put yourself in compromising situations where you will be face-to-face with the very thing you are trying to break free from.

THE APOSTLE PAUL'S TAKE

> "But now that you know God—or rather are known by God—how is it that you are turning back to those weak and miserable principles? Do you wish to be enslaved by them all over again?"
>
> (Galatians 4:9 NIV)

TAKE TWO

> "Be very careful, then, how you live—not as unwise but as wise, making the most of every opportunity, because to days are evil."
>
> (Ephesians 5:15-16 NIV)

CALLED TO DUTY: SPIRITUAL WARFARE

Unlike the popular video game "Call of Duty: Modern Warfare," our war is raged in the spiritual realm:

> "For the weapons of our warfare are not carnal, but mighty through God to the pulling down of strongholds."
>
> (2 Corinthians 10:4 NIV)

GET YOUR ARMOR

Every great soldier is prepared for battle. He'd never go to war without the proper equipment or protection unless he planned to fail.

APOSTLE PAUL'S ADVICE

> "Finally, be strong in the Lord and in his mighty power.

Put on the full armor of God so that you can take your stand against the devil's schemes.

"For our struggle is not against flesh and blood, but against the rulers, against the authorities, against the powers of this dark world and against the spiritual forces of evil in the heavenly realms.

"Therefore put on the full armor of God, so that when the day of evil comes, you may be able to stand your ground, and after you have done everything, to stand. Stand firm then, with the belt of truth buckled around your waist, with the breastplate of righteous in place, and with your feet fitted with the readiness that comes from the gospel of peace.

"In addition to all this, take up the shield of faith, with which you can extinguish all the flaming arrows of the evil one. Take the helmet of salvation and the sword of the Spirit, which is the word of God. And pray in the Spirit on all occasions with all kinds of prayers and requests.

"With this in mind, be alert and always keep on praying for all the saints."

(Ephesians 6:10-18 NIV)

In other words, get on your knees and fight like a man.

Teen Take

It's easy to make a habit of something. If you make reading the Bible a habit, you're arming yourself against the day's struggles. If you don't read it and don't pray, it's pretty much like bringing a knife to a gunfight.

There are times when I am tempted to do things I shouldn't. Being tempted is not a sin. Dwelling on it and then acting upon the temptation is! When I am tempted, there are two ways it will turn out: I either give in or I don't. I've noticed that when I'm constantly reading my Bible and praying to God every day, it's really a lot easier to say "No." When I'm not reading my Bible, I'm ten times more likely to take the bait. And in most cases I do.

I make a habit to read my Bible daily, but it's easy to fall out of that habit, making me vulnerable to attack.

My favorite verse is, "Resist the devil and he will flee!" (James 4:7).

Just resist! I don't need to hold a 15-round boxing match. I just have to make it look like he's really gonna have to work to bring me down. Then the devil runs away and will return another day. When tempted, pray to God—He will provide a way out! Distract yourself by reading the Bible. Remember: resist the devil and he will flee.

Truth about Prayer

REGENER8

Week 6 Day 1

WHY SHOULD I PRAY?

Prayer is communication between you and God, and like we discussed in Week 3, communication is vital to having a great relationship.

I love my children, and I want them to share their joys and sorrows with me. I want to hear how their day was. I want to know their hopes and dreams, likes and dislikes, and yes, even what they want for Christmas.

If my children didn't talk to me for months at a time, we wouldn't have a very good relationship. And they wouldn't have a very good Christmas, if you know what I mean.

THE BIBLE'S TAKE

> "If you remain in me (Jesus), and my words remain in you, ask whatever you wish, and it will be given to you."
>
> (John 15:7 NIV)

> "They will call on my name and I will answer them; I

will say, 'They are my people,' and they will say, 'The Lord is our God.'"

(Zechariah 13:9b NIV)

When people talk to God, He listens.

THAT'S IT?

I purposely kept this week's devotions on prayer short, because I want you to spend some time in prayer, specifically asking God to help you develop a meaningful prayer life.

Get to praying.

Week 6 Day 2

THE BIBLE TELLS ME SO

The main reason we should pray is because Jesus instructs and expects us to do so.

We pray out of obedience to the one who gave His very life for us.

When Jesus spoke about prayer, He said *when* you pray, not *if* you pray. Check out Matthew 6:5a.

ALWAYS PRAY.

> "Then Jesus told his disciples a parable to show them that they should always pray and not give up."
>
> (Luke 18:1 NIV)

DON'T STOP

> "Be joyful always, pray continually, give thanks in all circumstances, for this is God's will for you in Christ Jesus."
>
> (1 Thessalonians 5:16-18 NIV)

BE EFFECTIVE

"Do not be anxious about anything, but in everything, by prayer and petition, with thanksgiving, present your requests to God. And the peace of God, which transcends all understanding, will guard your heart and your minds in Christ Jesus."

(Philippians 4:6-7 NIV)

"The prayer of a righteous man is powerful and effective."

(James 5:16 NIV)

Now, go be effective. Pray.

Week 6 Day 3

WHAT SHOULD I SAY?

That's a great question. I'm glad you asked it. Jesus knew you'd be wondering, so He left us some instructions on how to pray.

DON'T KNOW ANY FANCY WORDS?

Good, 'cause you don't need them. Here's how Jesus feels about fancy words:

> "And when you pray, do not keep on babbling like pagans, for they think they will be heard because of their many words. Do not be like them, for your Father knows what you need before you ask him."
>
> (Matthew 6:7-8 NIV)

BOTTOM LINE?

Keep it real. Talk to God in a way that you feel comfortable.

DON'T MAKE A SCENE

> "And when you pray, do not be like the hypocrites, for they love to pray standing in the synagogues and

on the street corners to be seen by men. I tell you the truth, they have their reward in full. But when you pray, go into your room, close the door and pray to your Father, who is unseen. Then your Father, who sees what is done in secret, will reward you."

(Matthew 6:5-6 NIV)

That does not mean that you can't pray on the streets in your town. It's not so much *where* the people were praying but the *motive* behind the prayers. They were praying and creating a scene so that people would see them and think that they were really righteous and pure.

*Take some time to pray
for your friends today.*

Week 6 Day 4

DOES GOD RESPOND?

We've established the fact that God wants us to pray. We know how to pray and we know that God hears our prayers. But does He answer our prayers?

WHAT DOES JESUS SAY?

> "If you remain in me and my words remain in you, ask whatever you wish, and it will be given you."
>
> (John 15:7 NIV)

> "So I say to you: Ask and it will be given to you; seek and you will find; knock and the door will be opened to you. For everyone who asks receives; he who seeks finds; and to him who knocks, the door will be opened."
>
> (Luke 11:9-10 NIV)

I've personally had many prayers answered by God, and He has used me as a means to answer the prayers of others. (Remember the story of the woman and the groceries?)

BUT HE'S GOD, NOT A GENIE

God doesn't live in a little bottle that He pops out of when you rub it so He can grant you three wishes, which would probably be: 1) hot girlfriend, 2) millions in cash, and 3) muscles.

Jesus said, "*If you remain in me*." If you're living for Christ and serving Him, then you will ask for things to help you in those endeavors. Jesus will equip you with the things you ask for to accomplish His mission through you.

LET ME EXPLAIN

If my son asks me to help him get good grades, I'll help him because that's my will for him. If he asks me to help him do well in life, once again, my will for him.

If he asks for a bicycle, I'll reward him with one for doing well.

But if he asks me for a gun, the answer is no. I don't care how good a shot he is. My will is not for him to hurt himself.

SAME WITH GOD

"This is the confidence we have in approaching God: that if we ask anything according to His will, He hears us. And if we know that He hears us—whatever we ask—we know that we have what we asked of Him."

(1 John 5:14-15 NIV)

Spend some time today asking God what His will is for your life.

Additional reading: 1 John 3:22

Week 6 Day 5

QUALITY PRAYER LIFE

Today we'll cover some of the essentials for a quality prayer life. It's not an exhaustive list, but it covers the main points.

HUMBLE HEART = SUCCESSFUL PRAYER

> "If my people who are called by my name, will humble themselves and pray and seek my face and turn from their wicked ways, then I will hear from heaven and will forgive their sin and will heal their land."
>
> (2 Chronicles 7:14 NIV)

God gives us the conditions that we must follow in order for Him to hear us as well as answer our prayer. We just have to have the courage to follow them.

SEEK GOD WHOLE-HEARTEDLY

> "Then you will call upon me and come and pray to me, and I will listen to you. You will seek me and find me when you seek me with all your heart."
>
> (Jeremiah 29:12-13 NIV)

God doesn't want just a piece of us. He wants all of us. He doesn't want the leftovers. He wants the first fruits, the best of us.

> "Therefore I tell you, whatever you ask for in prayer, believe that you have received it, and it will be yours."
>
> (Mark 11:24 NIV)

HAVE FAITH

> "But when he asks, he must believe and not doubt, because he who doubts is like a wave on the sea, blown and tossed by the wind. That man should not think he will receive anything from the Lord; he is a double-minded man, unstable in all he does."
>
> (James 1:7 NIV)

> "And without faith it is impossible to please God, because anyone who comes to Him must believe that he exists and that he rewards those who earnestly seek Him."
>
> (Hebrew 11:6 NIV)

I'm gonna have a little faith myself and assume you get the idea. Faith is the backbone of Christianity.

ADD RIGHTEOUSNESS

> "Therefore confess your sins to each other and pray for each other so that you may be healed. The prayer of a righteous man is powerful and effective."
>
> (James 5:16 NIV)

Confess your sins ASAP.

LEARN OBEDIENCE

> "Dear friends, if our hearts do not condemn us, we have confidence before God and receive from him anything we ask, because we obey his commands and do what pleases him."
>
> (1 John 3:21-22 NIV)

When my kids obey me, I reward them. When they ask if they can go to the movies or the mall, I let them.

GOD'S REWARD PROGRAM

God rewards His children for obedience just as He disciplines them for disobedience.

Follow these guidelines, and you'll develop a meaningful and effective prayer life.

Week 6 Day 6

A MODEL FOR PRAYER

I figured it was a good idea to end a week focused on prayer by looking at the prayer Jesus gave us as a model:

> "This, then, is how you should pray:
> 'Our Father in heaven,
> Hallowed be your name,
> Your kingdom come,
> Your will be done,
> on earth as it is in heaven,
> Give us today our daily bread.
> And forgive us our debts,
> as we also have forgiven our debtors.
> And lead us not into temptation,
> But deliver us from the evil one.'"
>
> (Matthew 6:9-13 NIV)

A BLUEPRINT

Jesus didn't intend for this to be the only prayer we pray, but rather a blueprint, a guide, for our own prayers.

ACKNOWLEDGEMENT

"Our Father in heaven…."

This acknowledges the relationship between God and us. He is our Father, and He loves us. It also places Him in authority over us.

PRAISE

"Hallowed be your name…."

Show reverence and praise Him for who He is.

HIS WILL

"Your kingdom come. Your will be done on earth as it is in heaven." Choose His will over your own desires and plans.

OUR NEEDS

"Give us today our daily bread."

Only after we acknowledge and praise Him do we ask for things we need and would like to have. Acknowledge that He is our provider.

FORGIVENESS

"And forgive us our debts as we also have forgiven our debtors."

When we acknowledge our sin, He is faithful and just, and forgives us. We must forgive others as well.

LEADER

"Lead us not into temptation, but deliver us from the evil one…"

God does not tempt us, but He allows us to be tested. We ask for help and guidance from the Holy Spirit so that we can avoid situations and traps from the devil.

DON'T JUST DIAL 911

We don't like it when people only call us when they want some-thing, and God does not appreciate it when we only call on Him when we are in trouble or need something. If you follow the model of prayer that Jesus gave us, you'll be honoring God, and you'll probably see extraordinary results in your prayer life.

I pray that you, as a reader of this book, will experience a Christ-centered prayer life, that you will continue to grow in your relationship with Christ, and that your prayers will be answered according to God's will for your life.

Teen Take

I don't want to come across as some holier-than-thou spiritual guru. I've always struggled in my prayer life. I've been guilty many times of only talking to God out of need. Sometimes I'd pray as I was going to sleep, and I didn't get real far before I was out. I grew up saying the same prayer every night—the "now I lay me down to sleep" one.

It was just something my parents made me do, and it didn't really mean anything to me, but I guess it did to them. It was hard to talk to somebody I couldn't see; to be honest, it felt stupid. I didn't have a problem, though, if a minister was praying or something. It just didn't matter to me if I prayed or not.

Today it's a lot better. I listened to people talk about how they had the same issues but that they started making time to pray, and that God was answering their prayers and stuff. They also asked me what would happen if I talked to my girlfriend as little as I talked to God. What kind of relationship would we have? There probably wouldn't be a relationship.

Today I make an effort to pray for people—not just when I want something. I also try to remember to thank Him for stuff too.

Truth About Evangelism

REGENER8

Week 7 Day 1

EVANGELISM = FEAR

Want to strike fear in grown men? Want to see women sweat bullets? Just mention the words *witness* or *evangelism*, and that's enough to send most people running and crying in fear.

SOMETHING YOU LIVE

The reason the majority of people freak out at the thought of witnessing to their friends about Jesus is because they are wrongly taught that evangelism is something you *do*, when in fact it's something you *live*.

NUT JOBS

When I was a teenager, we went to the beach. As I was walking on the boardwalk, there was a guy holding up a sign and yelling at people that they were going to burn in hell if they didn't repent. Nobody took him seriously. Most people just laughed and thought he was crazy, and maybe he was just a nut job.

I decided right then and there that, no matter what, I was never going to witness to anyone.

JUST MEMORIZE THIS

My other experience with witnessing was just as bad.

My mom made me go to church and Sunday school and youth group.

I remember one Sunday night making my way to the damp church basement (that's where the youth group met), and being informed by the youth pastor that we would be role-playing.

We broke up into pairs and spent the next forty-five minutes pretending to "witness" to our partner.

The youth pastor gave us index cards with possible scenarios we might run into out in the "real world."

After all the "fun" ended, we were told we would be going out to the mall to try out what we just learned.

Say what? Oh, heck no! Somebody might see me, and I already don't have friends.

We were supposed to walk up to complete strangers and recite the things we'd memorized on those little cards: "Excuse me do you know that Jesus loves you and died for you and would you like to repeat this prayer after me then you can go to heaven too?" (Inhale.)

I couldn't wait to get bigger than my mom and quit church.

HERE'S SOME GOOD NEWS

Jesus never intended for us to "witness" like that.

I was relieved when I read the Bible and there was nothing in it describing the little youth group exercise. But I was also mad that I was led to believe that sharing Jesus with people required me to act unnatural.

That kind of evangelism alienated me as well as a lot of other kids. It was turned into a chore you did once a week whether you liked it or not. We had no rapport with these victims that we cornered while they were busy shopping.

SO HOW DO WE DO IT?

Just be you. Be genuine. When you treat people the way Jesus did, and you love others as yourself, people will be drawn to you. They'll see something in you that they want for themselves.

Here's how Jesus described it:

> "You are the light of the world. A city on a hill cannot be hidden. Neither do people light a lamp and put it under a bowl. Instead they put it on its stand, and it gives light to everyone in the house. In the same way, let your light shine before men, that they may see your good deeds and praise your Father in heaven."
>
> (Matthew 5:14-16 NIV)

This week we're going to talk about Relational Evangelism and what that looks like.

Don't worry.
There are no index cards involved.

Week 7 Day 2

WELCOME BACK

Good to see you. I was afraid you wouldn't be back when you found out we'd be talking about sharing your faith, especially after my youth group horror story.

DON'T WORRY

As promised, there are no index cards, no role-playing games, and no surprise trips to the mall. So relax and stop sweating.

JESUS IS THE ANSWER

I figured we'd start with why it's important to share our faith with others.

There are lots of hurting, broken people in this world who are searching for true peace and the answer to why they are here.And there are simply not enough people, not counting the role-players and burn-in-hell dudes, who are sharing Jesus with them. I'm not talking about a delusion of Jesus or a Hollywood version of Jesus. I'm talking about the Jesus of the Bible.

JESUS NEEDS MORE WORKERS

"Then he [Jesus] said to his disciples, 'The harvest is plentiful but the workers are few. Ask the Lord of the harvest, therefore, to send out workers into his harvest fields.'"

(Matthew 9:37-38 NIV)

Nothing has changed in 2,000 years. Few workers then, few workers now.

The world views the church as a social club filled with self-righteous, judgmental hypocrites. And sadly, for the most part, they are right.

WHAT'S IT GOING TO TAKE TO CHANGE THAT?

We need to stop trying to bring people to Jesus, and start taking Jesus to the people.

We do that, not by spouting off some script we memorized, but by living our faith out in front of them. Be kind and caring. Help your neighbors. Honor your commitments. Listen.

BE THE KIND OF PERSON THAT YOU WOULD WANT TO BE AROUND

Don't fake sincerity just to shove Jesus down their throat the first chance you get. Be sincere because you are.

Build genuine relationships with people, and you won't need a script because you'll be living your faith in front of them.

YOU'LL BE THE GENUINE ARTICLE

People will be drawn to you. The world is sick of the slick used-car salesman type. You'll be a refreshing unexpected change.

At first people may wonder what your angle is. But if you have really transformed your heart and mind, you won't need an angle.

Go be the hands and feet of Jesus.

Week 7 Day 3

RELATIONAL EVANGELISM

Relational evangelism is the process of developing meaningful relationships with other people.

Jesus was the master of relational evangelism. Crowds by the thousands were drawn to Him. They forsook food, shelter, and comfort to follow Him everywhere. They didn't care that it was 175 degrees outside, or that the ground was too hard to sit on. They didn't even care if they had enough to eat.

WHAT WAS JESUS' M.O.?

Jesus focused on three things: He genuinely cared about people, He met their needs, and He taught them in interesting and relevant ways.

By living this mission, Jesus left us with the model of relational evangelism.

12 MEN

Although Jesus dealt with thousands of people, He chose to pour Himself into the lives of twelve men, known as the Disciples or the Apostles.

You can probably relate to this. You have a lot of friends at school, and even more on Facebook® and Xbox Live®, but only a handful of really close friends know everything about you. The intimate stuff. The stuff you would never share with the others. It's your core group.

Jesus invested three years of His life with these twelve men. They were ordinary people, just like you and me.

He walked with them, laughed with them, and cried with them.

Jesus multiplied himself to the 12th power. These twelve men changed the entire world.

Once you realize that Jesus does not expect you to change every single person in the world, the pressure's off. Living your faith becomes something you enjoy instead of a chore you dread.

You can make a difference in your core group of friends and teach them to do the same.

IT WORKS FOR ME

I follow the same method Jesus used. I run a youth ministry called 252 Underground (252underground.com), which allows me the privilege of meeting hundreds of teenagers. I enjoy these weekly meetings, but I also have a group of teens that I consider my core group.

I've invested countless hours in these young guys. We live life together. We go to the movies or out to eat as a group. They come to my house every week for dinner. We play video games or board games.

I know everything about them, and they know everything about me.

We share our good times and the not so good times. I love these guys, and I know they love me.

I get to disciple these young guys by living out my faith with them.

LOOK OUT FOR THAT...

I've been to churches that have tried to get young people to say a prayer to go to heaven by telling them that they may be hit by a bus on the way home. If this has ever happened to you, I'm sorry. I promise you that those folks meant well, but Jesus wasn't really focused on getting you to pray a scripted prayer.

Jesus was more concerned with you becoming a disciple.

> "Therefore, go and make disciples of all nations, baptizing them in the name of the Father and the Son and the Holy Spirit."
>
> (Matthew 28:19 NIV)

EVANGELISM = DISCIPLESHIP

Jesus didn't separate evangelism and disciple-making. Making disciples was the whole point of evangelism.

We will use the rest of this week to explore why creating disciples is so important, what being a disciple looks like, and how you can disciple others.

Week 7 Day 4

GOOGLE® IT

I Googled® the word *disciple*, and the simplest meaning of the word is "follower."

Webster had this to say: "One who accepts and assists in spreading the doctrines of another." (Apparently I'm a disciple of Chick-fil-A®).

CRITICAL MASS

That's what Jesus was calling us to when He told us to make disciples of all nations. We personally cannot reach all nations, but if we invest in five people a year, at the end of the year we've created five disciples.

If we teach them to do as we've done, at the end of the second year there are 25 new disciples. Third year, 125 new ones. Fourth year, 625. Fifth year, 3,125. Sixth year, 15,625. Seventh year, 78,125. Eight year, 390,625. Ninth year, 1,953,125. Tenth year, over 9,765,625. By year 13, 1.2 billion disciples. (Remember these are only the numbers for the new disciples added each year. To get a grand total, you'd have to add up all the years together. But you get the picture.)

Those numbers increase dramatically if you disciple five more each year and continue the process.

DUPLICATION

When you look at these numbers, you can see why it's so important to create disciples and teach them to do the same.

When you duplicate yourself, you see how it becomes possible to reach all nations.

Getting someone to pray a prayer won't get the job done. If that's all you did, the process would look something like this: You get five people to say a prayer in a year. You do it again in year 2; now you're up to 10 prayer pray-ers. Year 3, 15. Year 4, 20. Year 5, 25. Year 10, you have a grand total of 50. No comparison. In 10 years, you'd reach 50 people. In 50 years, you'd only have 250.

Go and make disciples.

Week 7 Day 5

NO SECRET FORMULA

No two people are alike, so training disciples is not a mathematical equation.

THE KEY

Read your Bible, and get your friends reading the Bible for themselves.

I like this acronym for BIBLE: _B_asic _I_nstructions _B_efore _L_eaving _E_arth.

ONE SIZE FITS ALL

Though each person is different, people seem to find exactly what they are looking for in the Bible. The Spirit directs them to the verse they need to read.

I've spoken at churches, and afterward numerous people came up to me and said, "I needed to hear that," or "I felt like you were talking to me."

The Bible can make up for your lack of knowledge also.

SIDE NOTE

Why am I telling you how to make disciples in this book? You're just a teenager, right?

Because I believe in the importance of making disciples. I trust this book will have an impact on your faith (because I prayed for that), and if it has the impact on you that I prayed for, then you're going to be excited and want to start doing something, and making disciples is the best thing you can do.

SIMPLE PLAN

I'm not talking about the rock band. I'm talking about your plan to make disciples.

As you live your faith in front of your friends, they will start to wonder what's going on with you. Hopefully, some will join you in this journey, and they'll look to you as a leader.

Peter put it this way:

> **"Your godly lives will speak to them better than any words. They will be won over by watching your pure, godly behavior."**
>
> (1 Peter 3:1-2 NIV)

I've already told you how I live out my faith with a core group of teens. You'll do the same. You'll hang out with them. Eat with them. Go to the movies together. Same things you do now, but with a missionary's intent: as you go about doing these things, you'll look for natural ways to build up your friends' faith and encourage them in their journey.

You can lead them in a Bible study, or you can find a church with a great youth program and invite them.

You can also go to www.REGENER8.com for for tips and support.

Week 7 Day 6

SPIRIT GUIDE

I'm not talking about your fairy godparents or some New Age religion. I'm talking about God in Spirit, the Holy Spirit. As you surrender your life to obeying God and teaching others to do the same, the Holy Spirit we talked about will be your guide.

IN JESUS' WORDS

"If you love me, you will obey what I command. And I will ask the Father, and He will give you another Counselor and He will be will you forever."

(John 14:15-16 NIV)

"But the Counselor, the Holy Spirit, whom the Father will send in my name, will teach you all things and remind you of everything I have said to you"

(John 14:26 NIV)

ORDINARY TO EXTRAORDINARY

God uses ordinary people just like you and me to accomplish

extraordinary things by the power of His Spirit.

> "But you will receive power when the Holy Spirit comes on you; and you will be my witnesses in Jerusalem, and in Judea and Samaria, and to the ends of the earth."
>
> (Acts 1:8 NIV)

I rely on the Holy Spirit to reveal both God's will for my life and the plans by which I need to accomplish His will.

I've been asked to speak at churches and organizations many times, and I always worry because I know I'm not an eloquent speaker. But the Holy Spirit not only gives me just the right words to say but the ability to speak them effectively. People always approach me afterward and tell me what a great speaker I am. I laugh to myself because I know the words are not mine.

Jesus explained:

> "Do not worry about what to say or how to say it. At that time you will be given what to say, for it will not be you speaking, but the Spirit of your Father speaking through you."
>
> (Matthew 10:19-20 NIV)

If you've never experienced this, I know it sounds crazy. But trust me.

More importantly, trust God.

GPS

Today most people have GPS in their cars and on their cell phones. The Global Positioning System is extremely awesome—how did we ever get along without it?

It takes the hassle out of traveling, except when a GPS device messes up. Which is rare, but it does happen.

As followers of Christ, we get a GPS that never messes up. It's God's Personal Spirit. If we listen for His voice, we'll arrive at the destination God intended for us.

The Holy Spirit is the fuel that drives us and empowers us to live an abundant life in Christ.

**Don't run out of gas before
you reach your destination.
Fuel up daily with the Holy Spirit.**

Teen Take

I use to think that, in order to share Jesus with people, I'd have to approach them about it. If you've ever done that or had someone do it to you, it's awkward, isn't it? Not to mention the person you approach, nine out of ten times, is going to tune you out and treat you like a psych case. It's all in how you live—how you act when you're at work and when you're hanging out with friends—and having the integrity you claim to have as a Christian.

The one thing that really sparks people's curiosity is when I don't swear. On several occasions I've been able to share my faith with my co-workers because they want to know why I don't swear. Then they ask why I'm not out every Friday getting wasted and doing drugs. More often than not, they respect me for what I believe even if they don't believe themselves.

Instead of preaching, "you're going to hell," it's best to live out your faith. They'll know we are Christians by our love, not pointing fingers.

Signed,
H

Truth about Money

REGENER8

Week 8 Day 1

GIVE ME ALL YOUR MONEY

If you've ever watched TV evangelists, you might think that God wants you to send all your money to support their million-dollar homes and exotic sports cars—I mean their ministries.

Those guys aren't speaking for God. God doesn't want you to send your hard-earned cash to some slick dude on TV so he can send you a prayer hanky.

WHAT DOES GOD WANT?

You. Plain and Simple.

If you give all your money to God and fail to obey His commands and love your neighbor, you may as well have blown it on video games.

> "He [Jesus] answered, 'Love the Lord your God with all your heart, and with all your soul, and with all your strength, and with all your mind and love your neighbor as yourself.'"
>
> (Luke 10:27 NIV)

Here's the Bible's take:

> "If you love me, you will obey what I command."
>
> (John 15:16 NIV)

SHOW ME THE LOVE

According to Jesus, our obedience is proof of our love and devotion.

God wants your heart before your wallet because He knows when He has your heart, He has your wallet. Get it?

Additional reading: John 14:21, John 14:23, John 15:10, 1 John 2:3, 1 John 5:3, 2 John 1:6

Week 8 Day 2

YEA! PRESENTS

If you're like me, you can't wait until Christmas Day to see what you got. You're excited and filled with anticipation.

When I was a kid, I'd tear through twenty gifts in two minutes. I just couldn't wait to see what each package contained.

WHAT I KNOW NOW

Now that I have kids of my own, I still wake up excited, but for a different reason. I can't wait for them to see the gifts I bought.

Sometimes I can't even wait until Christmas to give them their gifts.

I love to see their faces and share in their joy. I may even be just a bit more excited than they are.

AH, NOW I GET IT

"The Lord Jesus himself said: 'It is more blessed to give than receive.'"

(Acts 20:35b NIV)

Until I had kids, I thought this verse was whacked, but my perspective has changed. I truly enjoy giving gifts to people more than receiving them.

Once you take the focus off your wants and desires, it has a profound effect on you, and you truly are blessed through giving.

Don't give 'til it hurts.
Give 'til you're blessed.

Week 8 Day 3

HAPPY TO GIVE

Yesterday I talked about how excited I am to give my kids presents. I'm sure you've experienced the same reaction with your parents.

They have that stupid smile on their faces (you know the look), and make you wait to open your present until the camera is ready.

GUILT TRIP

What if, instead of being happy to give you presents, they made you feel guilty about receiving the presents?

What if they told you about all the bills they couldn't pay because they HAD to buy you those stupid presents?

What if, instead of wearing a smile as you opened your gifts, they looked disgusted?

What if they reminded you of all the things they could've bought for themselves if they didn't have to spend their money on you?

RE-GIFT IT

Would you feel good about keeping the gifts, or would you tell them to keep them?

HEART CHECK UP

God cares about the condition of your heart when giving. That's what these verses mean:

> "Remember this: Whoever sows sparingly will reap sparingly, and whoever sows generously will reap generously. Each man should give what he has decided to give in his heart to give, not reluctantly or under compulsion, for God loves a cheerful giver."
>
> (2 Corinthians 9:6-7 NIV)

Give out of love not out of guilt.

Week 8 Day 4

TEST GOD

> "'Bring the whole tithe into the storehouse, that there may be food in my house. Test me in this', says the LORD Almighty, 'and see if I will not throw open the floodgates of heaven and pour out so much blessing that there will not be room enough to store it.'"
>
> (Malachi 3:10 NIV)

I've personally tested God in the area of giving, and He has always taken care of me.

There were times I felt God was telling me to give and my obedience would mean a bill would not get paid. I obeyed anyway and God provided the bill money through other means.

GOD'S ECONOMY

> "Give, and it will be given to you. A good measure, pressed down, shaken together and running over, will be poured into your lap. For with the measure you use, it will be measured to you."
>
> (Luke 6:38 NIV)

You can't out-give God. He doesn't just promise to pay you back; He takes it even further. God says He'll press it down and shake it together.

I got a visual example of this just yesterday. I went paint-balling with some teens, and I bought 2,000 paint balls.

I decided to share mine. As I went around dividing them up, the guys opened the hoppers on their guns all the way to the top. I poured the balls into their hoppers, but before I could move on, they shouted, "Wait!" Then they shook the gun and the paint balls settled. Just like that, there was more room. I'd fill it again, and they'd shake it. I'd fill it until the paint balls spilled over.

That's exactly what God has in mind.

Week 8 Day 5

MORE THAN MONEY

When the Bible speaks of giving, most people immediately think of it in the financial sense, but there is so much more to giving.

Yes, God requires us to give a tenth of our income to Him, but He also expects us to give our time to others in need. Friendship to the lonely. Comfort to the suffering. Hope to the lost. Love to the unlovable. Forgiveness to our enemies.

Give of yourself. Give from the heart.

IN JESUS' WORDS

"But I tell you who hear me: Love your enemies, do good to those who hate you, bless those who curse you, pray for those whose mistreat you. If someone strikes you on one cheek, turn to him the other also.

"If someone takes your cloak [jacket], do not stop him from taking your tunic [shirt].

Give to everyone who asks you, and if anyone takes what belongs to you, do not demand it back.

"Do to others, as you would have them do to you. If you love those who love you, what credit is that to you? Even 'sinners' love those who love them. And if you do good to those who do good to you, what credit is that to you? Even 'sinners' do that.

"And if you lend to those from whom you expect repayment, what credit is that to you? Even sinners lend to sinners, expecting to be repaid in full.

"But love your enemies, do good to them, and lend to them without expecting anything back. Then your reward will be great, and you will be sons of the Most High, [God] because he is kind to the ungrateful and wicked.

"Be merciful, just as your Father (God) is merciful."

(Luke 6:27-36 NIV)

That takes a lot of giving on our part, so much more than just our money. We're even called to give up our rights sometimes.

That may sound hard, but the permanent benefits outweigh the temporary discomfort.

Week 8 Day 6

GIVING = TRUST

Giving of yourself and your money shows God that you trust Him, and proves to others that you believe in what you preach.

> "Trust in the Lord with all your heart and lean not on your own understanding."
>
> (Proverbs 3:5 NIV)

IT'S ALL GOD'S

Everything I get comes from God, so when I give 10% to God, I'm just giving Him back what was already His.

I like to think of it as God overpaid me and just wants to see if I give it back.

> "For the earth is the Lord's and everything in it."
>
> (1 Corinthians 10:26 NIV)

DEVELOP AN ATTITUDE OF GRATITUDE

Being grateful for the things you've been blessed with it makes it so much easier to be a giver: "I wept because I had no shoes until I saw a man who had no feet" (ancient proverb).

HONOR GOD

"Honor the Lord with your wealth, with the first fruits of all your crops [stuff, money, jelly beans], then your barns will be filled to overflowing, and your vats will brim over with new wine."

(Proverbs 3:9-10 NIV)

TITHE = 10%

Tithes are required by God and equal 10% of our gross income. We give this out of a loving obedience.

OBEDIENCE VS. SACRIFICE

"Does the Lord delight in burnt offerings and sacrifices as much as in obeying the voice of the Lord? To obey is better than sacrifice, and to heed is better than the fat of rams."

(1 Samuel 15:22 NIV)

OFFERING OR TITHE?

I always thought offerings and tithing were the same thing, but I learned that the tithe is giving what we owe to God, and our offering is what we give beyond what we owe.

It's like when I do my taxes. I have to pay Uncle Sam what I owe, but then there is a little box I can check off if I want to donate a dollar to some campaign. I never know what to do in this situation. I want to say, "No way, dude, you already took enough," but then I think, "Will they audit me if I don't give them a buck?"

Decisions, decisions.

Teen Take

My dad always told me all the church wanted was your money so the pastor could have a big house, drive a nice car, and not have to get a real job. I believed him because that's what I saw from those TV preachers: all they ever talked about was that people needed to send money to them.

I know now that those guys probably aren't doing stuff for God with the money. But I can't base whether or not I give to God on them. I learned that we give to God because He gives to us. I know that giving may not always be money, either—it could be my time or my stuff to poor people.

I always feel good after I do something good for someone in need, too. Someday, when/if I have kids, I'm not gonna tell them the stuff my father told me. I'm going to tell them what the Bible says about giving.

Final Thoughts

LOVE'S THE ONLY RULE

As we part ways, I hope this book has done one of two things: either strengthened your faith or started you on a new journey with God. I also pray that you see others as God sees them and know that no matter what situation you are faced with, love's the only rule.

If you remember that, then you will never go wrong.

Praise for *Regener8:*

Regener8 is a right-on book for teens—and even for those who might be a little older. The short chapters with brief, meaningful takeaway thoughts help readers ponder the words they've just read.

—Cecil Murphey, writer or co-writer of more
than 100 books, including *90 Minutes in Heaven*
and *Gifted Hands: The Ben Carson Story.*

Made in the USA
Lexington, KY
29 October 2013